A Repetition of the Sound Doctrine
Concerning the True Presence of the Body and Blood of the Lord in the Supper

By Martin Chemnitz
In the Church of Braunschweig

Including a treatment by the same author that deals with the doctrine of the communicatio idiomatum

With an index of the main headings that are explained in this book

Leipzig
1561

translated by Rev. Paul A. Rydecki

Repristination Press
Malone, Texas

First edition, January 2021.

REPRISTINATION PRESS
716 HCR 3424 E
MALONE, TEXAS 76660

www.repristinationpress.com

ISBN 1-891469-79-7 (10)
9781891469794 (13)

Table of Contents

Chemnitz's Preface

To the most esteemed gentlemen, full of wisdom and virtue, to the consuls and the whole senatorial order, to the most famous republic of Braunschweig, and to the lords entrusted with her care:

In ecclesiastical conflicts, when dissensions arise concerning crucial teachings, one must proceed with a measure of religious caution, ever guarding against that frivolity which carries a person about to and fro, driven by every wind of doctrine, so that, either from the zeal of the parties involved, or from a petulant desire for strife, one now approves, now condemns a certain opinion that has not been sufficiently examined. As Hilary said concerning the Arians, "They establish and then reestablish their creeds on a yearly—no, on a monthly—basis." Instead, the rule of St. Paul must be observed: "Test all things; hold fast what is good" (1 The. 5:21). Indeed, the Thessalonians are commended in the Scriptures for this very thing, that when they heard Paul arguing against the form of doctrine that had been received in the synagogues at that time, they did not immediately embrace the teachings of Paul out of a foolish affection for novelty, but they diligently searched the Scriptures to see if the things he was saying were true. In 1 Tim. 1, Paul calls them "idle talkers" who deal only in assertions and do not know what they are talking about. As the Epistle of Jude also says, "Many speak evil of things they know nothing about." [v. 10]

For many years, therefore, I did not spend much time in trying to understand the arguments that are considered irrefutable by both sides in the Sacramentarian controversy, lest I should either condemn what I did not know or blindly embrace what I have not sufficiently examined, for, according to Paul's teaching, "everyone should be convinced in his own mind" (Rom. 14:5). But since, over the last several years, that unfortunate conflict has arisen anew, and in an even more dangerous manner than before, I have determined, both for the sake of my own conscience and, God willing, as a matter of the faithfulness that Paul requires in the ministers of the Church, that it would be personally beneficial for me, in the small measure that I am able, to take up this task and to assemble and comment on the main headings and basic principles of this controversy by putting something down in writing.

In fact, while exploring other areas of Christian doctrine, I have found that, in this way, one's diligence in learning is sharpened and one's judgment is more fully formed. What is more, while I was considering these things, some of the brothers encouraged me to take up this topic and treat it in public lectures.

And so I have taken this opportunity to gather certain memorable statements from the chief writings of those who embrace the understanding set forth in the Augsburg Confession and its Apology, in which I believe that the main headings of the whole controversy are comprehended. And since I did not wish to introduce anything new, but only to repeat the same old things, I have taken great care to preserve the pattern of doctrine that has been used, whether by the older or by the more recent writers whose authority is approved in our churches, not only in the broad headings themselves, but also in their pattern of speech.

Nor am I sorry for undertaking this task, for I have obtained its most bountiful fruit. I know that, by the blessing of God, I have been confirmed in the right understanding by formulating this more accurate treatment of the basic principles, and I have been fortified against the protests of the fanatics, however plausible they may be. In addition, I find that this diligence also helps me to teach, for, since it is not always easy to explain things to the more simple-minded by using the sources and the basic principles themselves and by examining them with extensive writings and speeches, the principal themes must be shown and explained to them in a simpler and more concise manner. I have also found, by the grace of God, that this method has sometimes proven beneficial for the erring lambs who have been bewitched by Zwinglianism.

I thought that I had obtained enough benefits from this task and did not plan on publishing anything, in spite of the requests some had made. But as I had at first collected these things for my own personal use, so now for several years I have held onto them, so that, if there should ever be a need for a clarification of what we believe about the Lord's Supper, I might be able to provide a true and simple—if not eloquent—explanation, opposing the adversaries with solid refutations drawn from authentic sources. But since others, to whom I properly attribute this authority, wanted to make the decision for themselves concerning the publication of the writings I had assembled, I committed the whole matter to God and to the Church, and even more willingly, because I know that I have established nothing new. I have merely recited the pattern of sound doctrine simply and faithfully, and these consistent repetitions of the same confession are hardly useless. In addition, this, too, I have noticed: that some people are secretly nibbling away at this Church of ours with slander and false accusations, as if we were spewing forth any number of absurdities about the Lord's Supper. Indeed, I hope that any such reminders might be advantageous for showing the more simple-minded a simple "fisherman's method" (as Ambrose likes to say) with which they may be able, God-willing, to educate themselves in the face of all corrupt influences and to rest in a simple, quiet assurance, which is essential in all matters of faith.

I wanted to write and dedicate this work to you, most excellent gentlemen, as it has been composed from within your own Church, so that all who read it may know that there is in this state, by God's blessing, a beautiful relationship between the republic and the Church, which is surely pleasing to God and salutary to many consciences, for the Holy Spirit praises and commends it in Psalm 47, "The princes of the peoples have gathered together with the people of the God of Abraham." In the same way, it displeases Him when the opposite is true. He not only condemns the rulers who persecute His people, but He also rebukes that idleness that exists among the magistrates who do not care what sort of doctrine is set before the people. For in Judges 17, the cause of the depraved doctrine and of the corruption of the divine worship is described in this way: "In those days, there was no king in Israel. But each one did what seemed right to him." But your republic, by God's blessing, enjoys this notable dignity and splendor for which it is rightly praised, that, with its utmost diligence and its just severity, it is the guardian of an honorable discipline. And then this surpassing gift has also been added, that your republic kisses the Son of God and serves Him with fear and trembling, as Psalm 2 declares, and that it nurses the Church, according to that sweet oracle of Isaiah. God has also given clear testimonies of His blessing upon your republic, in that, in the midst of all the chaos that plagues the nations, He has preserved among you a reasonable measure of order. And in the face of so many and grievous distractions and dissensions, He has granted and maintained a pious concord among the teachers and learners in this Church, of which I rejoice to be a citizen and member.

Therefore, I ask the Son of God, our Lord Jesus Christ, that He would perpetually grace this republic and Church with these great blessings, which are really His own heavenly gifts, for the glory of His name and for the edification of the Church.

Presented in Braunschweig on the 3rd day of March, AD 1560.

Your most devoted Martin Chemnitz,
Minister of the Church of Braunschweig

Mörlin's Preface

To the pious reader: Grace and peace through Christ.

My dear coadjutor, Master Martin Chemnitz, prepared this treatment of the Lord's Supper primarily for his own personal use, so that he might strengthen his conscience and, if necessary, be able to provide his own response to this great controversy, not with the futile and frigid reasoning of the foolish flesh or with the fabricated and finely dressed conclusions of inane philosophy, but with the true foundations, drawn from the authority of God's Word and of purer antiquity, and in perpetual agreement with the doctrine of Luther, the man of God. However, when I realized that this labor of his would be beneficial and salutary for the Church of Christ, I did not stop pressing, urging, and imploring Him for Christ's sake not to bury this talent in the ground, but to place this lamp on a lampstand, that it may also give light to many others in the house of the Lord. After many pleas and even some annoying harassment, my request has finally been granted.

You will find nothing here, dear Christian reader, about a local inclusion; nothing about transubstantiation; nothing about an immense and infinite ubiquity of the body of Christ—although our church in this illustrious city was shamelessly defamed and discredited last year when unjust charges were brought against us for this. If we wanted to answer these charges here, we would certainly be able to provide a worthy response. But we will forego these things for the common tranquility, lest anyone should add to the false accusations.

We retain in our church the pattern of sound words which Christ, the Son of God, used from the beginning when He instituted His Supper and which He wanted and commanded us to use. We say that the bread, after the blessing is received, or after the prayer of the Word, as Justin and others speak, is the body of Christ. But lest anyone think that we are playing with an ambiguity of words, as the chief actors now tend to do, we add that clarification which we have in the words of Christ, namely, that we understand "body," not for a power or efficacy or association, or for a sign of the body, but for that substance or essence which hung on the altar of the cross and was sacrificed by our High Priest, Jesus Christ, for the redemption of the whole human race. Therefore, we reject and condemn the madness of all the Sacramentarians, who, for no other reason than that they are unable to comprehend and measure the power of God with their own foolish reasoning, shroud the manifest and clear words of Christ in their own darkness, and snatch them away into another sense, so that they deceitfully rob us of the testament of the Son of God, and with it, this most sacred treasure.

Also of great benefit is the piety and vigilance of our excellent senate, which restrains men of this kind who blaspheme against the words of Christ, if they refuse to yield to any salutary and pious admonitions, allowing themselves to be corrected from the Word of God and led back onto the path, lest one diseased sheep should infect and ruin the whole sheepfold of Christ.

But since we also wish to confess publicly that we disapprove and condemn the papistic transubstantiation, we explain this statement, that the bread is the true body of Christ, with these formulae which have been confirmed and received by much use and by antiquity: The body of Christ, which was given for us, is truly and substantially present with the bread, in the bread, or under the bread. For in this way antiquity, Luther, and all the sound teachers of the churches in this age of ours have spoken, together with St. Paul himself, who said, "The bread that we break is the communion of the body of Christ." That is, when the bread is distributed and received, the body of Christ is, at the same time, truly distributed and received, not only by the believing heart, but also by the mouth, as Augustine said.

But Master Martin has written sufficiently in this treatise about our doctrine and the unanimous consensus of this Church. For this is what we believe and teach, as he himself has written, and in this consensus of ours, God-willing, we will persevere with a simple heart against all the madness of all the Sacramentarians, against all the charges of our detractors, and, finally, against every height that exalts itself against the knowledge of God. We shall persevere only by the grace of Him who said, "No one will snatch them from My hand." We fervently implore Him to preserve us unblemished with this Church in purity of doctrine, as we have received it through the Rev. Dr. Martin Luther, the man of God. Amen.

Joachim Mörlin

Preface to the 2020 Translation

That the treasure which is Martin Chemnitz's 1561 work concerning the Sacrament of the Altar, *Repetitio sanae doctrinae,* has remained untranslated until now is a powerful reminder of how much work remains to be done in the task of translating the Lutheran Fathers into the English language. Several generations have passed since the late Dr. J.A.O. Preus translated one of Chemnitz's later works on the same topic, and much of the recent secondary literature has been written from the ill-considered assumption that this later work somehow supplanted the several works which Chemnitz had already written on the topic. Such assumptions have done a disservice to the study of both the theologian and his writings on this important theological locus.

The present volume was written during a critical phase of the struggles to come to a clear and thorough confession concerning the Sacrament of the Altar within the Evangelical Lutheran Church after the death of Martin Luther and the travails of the Smalkaldic War and resultant Interim, and the subterfuges and calumnies of certain theologians. The situation had reached such an appalling point that as Philip Melanchthon was awaiting death, he rejoice that departing to be with the Lord would deliver him from the "*rabies theologorum*"—the madness of the theologians.

The immediate impetus for the writing and publication of *Repetitio sanae doctrinae* was the charge that had been made against Superintendent Joachim Mörlin (somewhat ironically, by Melanchthon) that Mörlin's views concerning the consecration of the sacred elements inclined toward Transubstantiation and *artolatreia* ("bread worship"). Throughout the *Repetitio,* Chemnitz clarifies what has been the consistent Lutheran position regarding the Sacrament, establishing the orthodoxy of that understanding from Holy Scripture, and extensively documenting that the Lutheran position is wholly consistent with the doctrine of the Church Fathers. Toward this end, several of the chapters are of particularly critical importance. For example, in chapter XXI, Chemnitz explains the proper understanding of the veneration of the Holy Sacrament. In chapter XXXI, he places the controversies of his day in light of the whole course of Church history. Chapter XXXII anticipates his profoundly significant contribution to the field of Christology, his monumental *De Duabus Naturis in Christo* (*Concerning the Two Natures in Christ*).

Later works, such as the aforementioned one translated by Preus, were oriented primarily toward a refutation of Reformed attacks on the Scriptural doctrine concerning the Lord's Supper. Certainly a similar concern animates the *Repetitio*, as well. However, the primary emphasis in this work is a defense of the authentic understanding of the Sacrament within the Evangelical Lutheran Church. Quite often, Chemnitz prudently framed his line of argumentation in terms of the Zwinglians and other Reformed teachers, but the work (particularly in its early chapters) is aimed more toward defining the discussion within Lutheran circles rather than simply refuting the Reformed. Thus, when read in conjunction with works such as Chemnitz's last book on the Holy Sacrament, one may gain a more balanced understanding of the thought of the 'second Martin' regarding this critical locus. The reader is given insights into Chemnitz's brilliance as a theologian at a relatively early point in his service in the office of the holy ministry.

Rt. Rev. James D. Heiser, M.Div., S.T.M.
Bishop, The Evangelical Lutheran Diocese of North America

The Festival of the Conversion of St. Paul, A.D. 2021

Repetition of the Sound Doctrine Concerning the True Presence of the Body and Blood of the Lord in the Supper

True and necessary is that distinction which Augustine also uses: The question about the substance of the Sacrament is one thing; the question about the power and efficacy, the true use and benefit of the Sacrament, is another, just as there is one debate about the person of Christ, and another about His offices. And just as the heretics of old who did not judge rightly concerning the person of Christ would argue strenuously about His offices so that their wickedness might be peddled the more securely under the guise of piety, so the Zwinglians contend that there is no cause for quarrelling if dissensions arise in the Church over the substance of the Lord's Supper, as long as the other issue concerning its benefit and efficacy remains intact and is rightly taught. But since the Son of God has revealed both things to us in the Word—how the substance and how the true benefit of His Supper are to be understood—we properly affirm, as Christ says in another place, that the latter is to be done without omitting the former. Therefore, that doctrine concerning the true use of the reception in the Lord's Supper is rightly taught in its place in our churches, and indeed, it is carefully inculcated with frequent repetition. But this present treatise is primarily directed toward the other part, concerning which there have now broken out again the most grievous contentions, concerning the substance of the Lord's Supper: what is present, offered, and received with the bread and wine in the Supper, when the words of the Son of God affirm, "This is My body. This is My blood."

I wanted to mention these things about the argument from the outset, lest some blasphemer bring the charge (as they are wont to do) that, by carelessly ignoring that important doctrine concerning the true benefit of the Eucharist, we are only promoting unnecessary contentions about that other issue.

I. Is the controversy about the Lord's Supper similar to those debates in which different opinions do not impede the soundness of the faith?

Many people like to philosophize that this controversy is not an article of faith, and so, if a person retains a foundation in the necessary articles of faith, and if a remembrance and proclamation of the death of Christ is made in the Supper, then those words—"This is My body, this is My blood"—can, without danger to faith or detriment to salvation, be dragged away and explained according to various understandings, whether this, or that, or in a thousand different ways, however you want. And in that diversity of understandings, one has the pure and true Lord's Supper no less than the other. Indeed, almost as with a trumpet signal, the impudence of crafting infinite opinions is stirred up and increased in profane minds, as happened with Pelagius. When he was convicted by testimonies of Scripture, he began to claim that whatever anyone thought about original sin was a matter of rhetorical debate, not a matter of faith or of heresy.

Right from the beginning, then, it must be always be diligently impressed and carefully considered that the controversy over the Lord's Supper is not the same kind of dispute as one finds in the *Historia Tripartita,* where someone said "footstool" instead of "couch," or like the debates over the kikayon plant mentioned in Jonah 4, where each one can follow his own conjectures freely and without danger to faith and salvation, embracing the opinion that he views to be the more probable. For the one who interprets it as "ivy," as do Aquila and Symmachus, does not sin; nor is the one who understands it as a "gourd plant" subject to judgment. Nor would it be right for a person to accuse the Septuagint of heresy because they translated it κολοκύνθην, "pumpkin."

Jerome's detractors are deservedly reprimanded for hurling the charge of sacrilege against him in Rome because he had translated the word as "ivy" instead of "gourd." And they are rightly ridiculed who, in Africa, incited the revolt of the gourd and forced the president of the Church to restore it to "gourd" instead of "ivy." No, the reader can follow his own conjectures and embrace a different explanation than everyone else. He can understand a white grapevine or a wild turnip, and even this difference of opinions does no harm whatsoever to the soundness of faith.

But in this present controversy, things are very different. For Paul uses the strongest possible words when he says that the judgment of eternal condemnation and the guilt of the Lord's body and blood are attached, if a person does not discern the body of the Lord. And if the body of the Lord is to be discerned in the Supper, then the knowledge of those words—"This is My body"—must of necessity come before the discerning. If this knowledge or understanding is not true, then the discernment cannot rightly be made, and thus the horrible sentence will follow, "He eats judgment on himself." Likewise, "He will be guilty of the Lord's body and blood." So, then, it is by no means a harmless thing for clever men to have toyed with these words, "This is My body, etc."

With these true and serious warnings the petulance of clever men must be blunted when they begin to play around with their made-up, foreign, and cleverly-devised interpretations, for it is a terrible thing to fall into the judgment of God and to incur the guilt of the body and blood of the Lord. Cyprian applies this elegantly to that passage in Matthew 5, "Whoever breaks one of these smallest commandments, etc." For he says, "Therefore, it is a much worse thing to break one of these great commandments that pertain to the very Sacrament of the Lord's suffering and of our redemption, or to change it by human tradition."

II. Repetition of the doctrine and understanding of those churches which confess the true presence of the body and blood of the Lord in the Supper; that pattern of words which is found in the public confessions.

Once a consensus in doctrine has been established, it is also useful for a whole host of reasons to maintain and preserve a definite pattern of sound words, and it is a matter of worthy diligence for those who have been piously instructed to speak as one with the Church for the sake of concord, lest there should daily arise new confessions which are not as felicitously written. I have, therefore, compiled several formulas which are found in the public confessions of our churches.

In the Augsburg Confession:

> Concerning the Lord's Supper, they teach that the body and blood of Christ are truly offered with the bread and wine to those who eat and drink in the Lord's Supper.

In the Apology of the Confession:

> The Tenth Article has been approved in which we confess our opinion that the body and blood of Christ are truly and substantially present in the Lord's Supper, and are truly offered with the visible elements of bread and wine to those who receive the Sacrament. Our preachers have continually defended this opinion. And we are well aware that not only the Roman Church affirms the bodily presence of Christ, but that the Greek Church now believes and long ago believed the same thing, as the Canon of the Mass used among the Greeks testifies. There are also the testimonies of various writers. For Cyril says, on John 15, that Christ is offered to us bodily in the Supper. This is what he says: "While we do not deny that we are joined spiritually to Christ by genuine faith and sincere love, we emphatically deny that there is no way for us to be joined to Him according to the flesh, and we

declare that to be entirely foreign to the divine Scriptures. For who ever doubted that Christ is also the vine in this way, and we the branches, who obtain life for ourselves from Him? Listen to Paul, who says: 'For we are all one body in Christ, because, though we are many, yet we are one in Him, for we all share in the one bread.' Or does he perhaps think that the power of the mystical blessing is unknown to us? And since this takes place in us, does it not also, by means of the communion of the flesh of Christ, cause Christ to dwell in us bodily?" And a little later: "Whence it must be considered that Christ is not only understood to be in us through love, but also by natural participation, etc."

We have not cited these things here in order to begin a debate over this topic, for the Imperial Majesty does not reject this article. No, we have done it so that whoever reads these things may also perceive more clearly that we defend the opinion that has been accepted in the whole Church, that in the Lord's Supper, the body and blood of Christ are truly and substantially present and are truly offered with the visible elements of bread and wine. And we speak about the presence of the living Christ, "For we know that death no longer has dominion over Him."

In the Formula of Concord[1], concerning the Sacramentarian affair, 1536:

They confess, in accord with the words of Irenaeus, that the Eucharist consists of two things, one earthly and the other heavenly. Therefore, they believe and teach that the body and blood of Christ are truly and substantially present, offered, and received with the bread and wine. And while they deny that transubstantiation takes place, and do not believe that a local inclusion occurs in the bread, or that there is any lasting union outside of the use of the Sacrament, nevertheless they grant that the Sacrament is

1 Note: the reference is to the Wittenberg Concord of 1536; the document now known as the Formula of Concord, which is included in the Book of Concord (1580), would not be written until 1577. (ed.)

the body of Christ by means of a sacramental union. For outside of the use, when it is kept in a pyx or displayed in processions, as is done by the Papists, they believe that the body of Christ is not present. Additionally, they believe that the institution of the Sacrament in the Church is valid and does not depend on the worthiness of the minister or the recipients. For this reason, just as Paul says that the unworthy also eat, so they believe that the body and blood of Christ are truly distributed also to the unworthy, and that the unworthy receive them, wherever the words and institution of Christ are observed. But such people receive them for judgment, as Paul says, for they abuse the Sacrament when they use it without repentance and faith. For the Sacrament was set forth for this reason, as a testimony that the benefits of Christ are applied to those who repent and comfort themselves by faith in Christ, and that such persons are washed in the blood of Christ.

In the Smalcald Articles:

Concerning the Sacrament of the Altar, we believe that the bread and wine in the Supper are the true body and blood of Christ. And we believe that His body and blood are distributed and received not only by the good Christians, but also by the evil.

In the Colloquy of Ratisbon of 1541, this formula was composed by our people:

Christ says, "Take, eat; this is My body. Drink; this is My blood." Therefore, we confess and teach that, in the Lord's Supper, the body and blood of the Lord are really and truly present with the bread and wine and are offered to the recipients. Thus Paul also says: "The bread that we break, is it not a participation in the Lord's body?" Therefore, we reject those who fail to confess the true presence of the body and blood of the Lord, and we hold to that which the Gospel teaches and which the holy Fathers confess. As Hilary says, "By the Lord's profession and by our faith, it is truly flesh and truly blood. And when they are taken and consumed, they cause Christ to be in us and us to be in Christ." And Chrysostom, "Christ joins Himself to each and every believer through this mystery, and wondrous mysteries are given to us so that we are His members, of His flesh and of His bones." Therefore, since Christ's body and blood are offered, Christ is present and is efficacious in us. This confession of ours testifies sufficiently that we retain the true and catholic understanding taught in the Gospel and among the ancient Fathers, etc.

Finally, I will add a brief and scholarly definition of Luther which embraces the entire matter brilliantly:

> The Sacrament of the Altar is the true body and the true blood of our Lord Jesus Christ, under the bread and wine, instituted by Christ Himself for us Christians to eat and to drink.

III. Concerning ubiquity.

There have been many debates about this question, and as usually happens, the minds of simpler people are disturbed by foreign arguments, and the chief matters are obscured. Therefore, I will write down Luther's brief and plain understanding of this matter, which is found in the eighth volume of Jena, page 375, which I have translated word for word in the simplest way possible.

"The true body and blood of Christ are given to be eaten and drunk in bread and wine. The question now arises, how can Christ be bodily in the Sacrament, since one body cannot be in many places at once?

"This is how I respond to that question: Christ said that He would be present there. Therefore, He is truly present in the Sacrament, and indeed, bodily so. Nor is another manner of His bodily presence to be sought than that which these words declare. Therefore, it must necessarily happen as the words declare. As for what pertains to the body, Christ can be wherever He wants, whenever He wants, even in all places, because there is a difference between the manner in which His body and our bodies function. One should not argue over ubiquity; that is a far different matter in this controversy. Nor do the scholastic teachers say anything here about ubiquity, but they retain the simple understanding of the bodily presence of Christ." Thus far Luther.

He says the same thing in his *Maior Confessio,* that in the Sacramentarian controversy, he does not wish to contend with anyone concerning ubiquity. His words are found in the second volume of Wittenberg, page 187.

IV. Concerning the mode of the presence of the true body and blood of Christ in the Supper.

Human curiosity has investigated and rashly affirmed many things also concerning this question. The Scholastics pretend that the body of Christ is present by a conversion or transubstantiation of the bread, just as the wine was present at Cana by the conversion of water. Indeed, the gloss, *De consecra. distin.* 2, says, "As soon as the outward form is ground away by the teeth, the body of Christ is snatched up into heaven." Since the Zwinglians cannot grasp or comprehend with reason how the very substance of the body and blood of Christ are present in the Supper, they speak only of the vigor, power, and efficacy of the absent body, just as the body of the sun, though it exists in a definite place in the heavens, is said by virtue of its rays and its effects to be on the earth, on the sea, etc.

Others imagine for themselves other modes of presence. Therefore, I have written down several statements in which this question is explained clearly, rightly, and consistently with the analogy of faith. Luther says the following in a certain letter to the Swiss, as I have translated it verbatim. "Concerning the Sacrament of the body and blood of Christ, we have never taught nor do we now teach that Christ descends from heaven or from the right hand of God, or that He ascends, either visibly or invisibly. For we steadfastly retain the article of faith, 'He ascended into heaven, sits at the right hand of God, from where He will come, etc.' And we commend it to divine omnipotence how His body and blood are given and offered to us in the Supper, where the institution is observed and executed according to His command. We do not think, nor do we speak, as if an ascent or a descent took place there, but we very simply retain His words, 'This is My body. This is My blood.'"

Brenz, Homily 50, *De Passione*: "When we say that the body and blood of Christ are present and distributed with the bread and wine in the Lord's Supper, one should not understand a mathematical presence. For mathematical ideas, concerning smallness or largeness, pertain to the affairs of this age, not to spiritual and heavenly affairs. Therefore, when it is said that the body and blood of Christ are contained in, and distributed with, the bread and wine according to the word of Christ, one should understand that the true body and the true blood of Christ are truly present, not in a mathematical or natural mode, but in a supernatural and heavenly one." Likewise: "The body and blood of Christ are truly and presently offered and distributed to us in the bread and wine of the Lord's Supper. And they are present, not by human power, but by the word and ordinance of our Lord Jesus Christ, who says whatever He wishes and is able to do whatever He says in heaven and on earth."

Luther in his *Confessio Minor*: "We teach that the body of Christ is in the Sacrament, not locally like straw in a sack or like wine in a cask, but definitively. That is, it is certainly present there, not like straw in a sack, and yet bodily and truly."

Pomeranus: "But how the body and blood of Christ are here, I believe that no one can know, nor should anyone be anxious to know it, since it is not understood from the word of Christ, nor are we commanded to understand it, but simply to believe what

Christ says and to do what He commands. This is a sufficient response to the institution of Christ."

Cyril has some pious, weighty, and elegant things to say on that passage in John 6: "How can He give us His flesh, etc.? Having learned our lesson from the mistake of others, let us not ask 'how' when God does His work. But let us grant to Him alone the path and the knowledge of His own work." Likewise: "Wherefore it behooved us rather to believe Christ. And if anything seemed challenging, we should have humbly sought an answer from Him instead of going about like drunken men exclaiming, 'How can He give us His flesh?' Do you not see that, when you say such things, a great arrogance is immediately revealed with those words?"

Likewise: "Let us, who place firm faith in the mysteries, never think or even mention that word 'how?' in such sublime matters, for this is a Jewish word."

V. What sort of predication or proposition is, "This is My body"?

If this declaration is soberly and rightly used, it sheds a great deal of light on many arguments in this whole controversy. For it uncovers many insidious deceptions, refutes many virulent calumnies, and shows the sources and the bases of the teaching concerning modes of speaking, of which more will be said later.

In the first place, it is clear and certain that this is no ordinary predication that corresponds to a certain mode of the five predicables. For the sense is not that the substance of the body of Christ—the price at which we were redeemed—is a lump of wheat, kneaded with water, formed by the hand of a baker and baked in an oven, etc. Nor is the sense that the blood that was shed for the remission of sins is the juice squeezed from the fruit of the vine. But just as the matter itself is a mystery that far exceeds the common course of nature and the capacity of reason, so also the saying is not subject to the ordinary modes of predicables.

In the second place, Zwingli's comment that this proposition is like others, such as, "The field is the world, the seed is the Word of God, etc.," is already indisputably rejected by the adversaries themselves. For in the institution of the Supper, there is no telling of a parable whose explanation is, "This is My body," as in Matthew 13.

Therefore, it is even more shameful that they have dared to draw a comparison between this statement and the one in Genesis 41, "The seven cows are seven years." For the minds of all the godly shudder to think that the most holy institution of the Supper should be compared to the telling of a dream, as if those words, "This is My body; this cup is the New Testament in My blood, etc.," were spoken in a dream!

Third. Schwenckfeldt philosophizes that the saying, "This is My body," is spoken in the same way as Ezekiel 5, where it says, in the riddle of the hairs that were set on fire and dispersed, that, "This is Jerusalem." And in Ezekiel 37, "These bones are the whole house of Israel." There are many examples like these in Zechariah 4 and 5, where the visions are explained in this way. But these are so clearly different from the words of the Supper that, among men of sound mind, there is no need for a refutation.

Fourth. There are figurative expressions: "I am the vine; you are the branches." "My Father is the farmer." "Beware of the yeast of the Pharisees." "Herod is a fox." But the proposition under discussion certainly does not follow the same reasoning as those. "The bread is the body of Christ," is not the same kind of statement as, "Herod is a fox."

It is well-known that, after the true and proper meaning has been abandoned, the things predicated in figurative expressions take on a new and metaphorical meaning due to a certain similarity. But as we shall soon demonstrate, unless we wish to rave with

Marcion and the Manichaeans that it was a ghost-like or figurative body that was given for us, neither can we nor should we include this proposition among the figurative expressions, for the phrase is added, "which is given for you." Therefore, just as the body of Christ hanging on the cross has the quality of a substance, so also in the Supper, for He says that it is that same body which is given for you.

Fifth. A clear distinction must be made between the two statements, "God is man," and, "This is My body." For it is not a personal or inseparable union that is to be understood of the bread and the body, as there is such a union between the divinity and the humanity in the person of Christ.

Sixth. The Papists pretend that the statement is identical where the same thing is predicated of itself. For they teach that the substance of the bread departs and is annihilated, being converted and changed into the body of Christ, and thus the bread is the body, just as, in Exodus 7, the staff of Moses is a serpent; or in John 2, the water in the jars is wine. In other words, the things which once were, namely, staff and water, have now been converted and changed into serpent and wine, etc. But this conclusion disagrees both with Paul and with the ancient writers, and there is a great dissimilarity between these examples. For in Exodus 7, after the conversion, there appears before the eyes, not the form of a staff, but of a serpent. And in John 2, the taster judges and concludes that it is wine, not water. This is not the case in the Eucharistic bread. Therefore, the examples are not alike.

Seventh. Since, then, the body is predicated of the bread and the blood of the wine, but not in any of those modes which we have mentioned, Luther skillfully and helpfully compares this proposition with these and similar statements. In Luke 3, the Holy Spirit descended upon Christ in bodily form as a dove. Psalm 104, "Who makes His angels winds and His ministers a flame of fire." In Acts 2, the Holy Spirit came upon the Apostles in a violent sound and in tongues of fire. John 20, "Christ breathed on them and said,

'Receive the Holy Spirit, etc.'" Yet we should not imagine that these things are exactly the same; as Damascenus said, "If the likeness differs in nothing from the thing itself, then it is not a likeness, but the thing itself." Nor, based on the comparison and similarity of those statements, should anything be added to those words, "This is My body," as many do, but the institution should always be and remain the foundation and the rule from whence the sense of those words can and should truly and safely be sought. For the Scripture itself clearly reveals a difference. In John 1 it says, "like a dove," and in Acts 2, "like fire." But here it simply says, "This is My body; this is My blood."

Therefore, we must consider why the comparison is established with these propositions rather than with others. And we should observe what the reasons are for the similarity and for the consistency, insofar as they agree simply and without sophistication with the words of institution, for such an examination will be helpful for clarifying many aspects of this controversy. We shall note, moreover, the chief parts of the similarity in this comparison of propositions.

First. Just as the Holy Spirit was not converted into the nature of a dove, nor are the flames in the mouth of the Apostles transubstantiated into the third person of the Trinity, so in this Sacrament there are and there remain two different things, without conversion or transubstantiation: the earthly element, that is, bread and wine; and the heavenly, that is, the body and blood of our Lord Jesus Christ.

Second. Just as the dove was a symbol, not only of the vigor and efficacy of the Holy Spirit, but also of His true and substantial presence, and yet no personal union was made, nor a local inclusion, nor an inseparable joining or circumscription, so the body of Christ is truly and substantially present with the bread, yet not as straw in a sack, etc.

Third. In those propositions which we are comparing, the visible things are either signs or symbols or figures (if we may call them that) of invisible things, but in such a way that the dove does not signify the absent Holy Spirit, nor is the flame of fire in Psalm 104 a symbol of the angelic nature which is disconnected therefrom through an interval of space. No, the things that are signified with those signs are truly and substantially present and offered. For the Holy Spirit, who is present everywhere, declared His own peculiar presence by means of those symbols (John 1, Acts 2).

In the same way, antiquity called the bread and wine "signs, symbols, and figures." Likewise, they used the words "signify, represent, point to, etc." And yet they all unanimously affirm that the body and blood of the Lord are truly and substantially present, offered, and received together with the things which are seen; namely, bread and wine.

Fourth. Just as John says that he saw the Holy Spirit descend when he saw the dove, so also those two separate things in the Eucharist, the bread and the body, come together as one and are joined together in such a union that, in the use of the Sacrament, where the bread is, there also is the body of Christ truly present, so that the body is predicated of the bread.

Fifth. In those propositions about the dove, about the tongues of fire, etc., there is no need to imagine figures of speech in the words; the terms retain their proper and native meaning. The dove in John 1 has the same meaning as it had at the time of the Flood (Gen. 8). Nor does the term "Holy Spirit" receive a new or metaphorical meaning; it means the same thing as when the Spirit of the Lord was hovering over the waters in Genesis 1. But the function of the predication is peculiar, which they call "unusual" (*inusitatam*), when an invisible thing, which is understood by the predicate, is signified as truly and substantially present with the visible subject. Thus in the Eucharist the nature of the bread remains. The "body" signifies that substance which was given on the cross for us. But the linking verb "is" signifies such a union of subject and predicate that, together with those things which are seen (bread and wine), the body and blood of Christ are truly and substantially (though invisibly) present and offered to those who eat. Luther calls this mode of speaking "synecdoche" (*Contra Carlstadt*, fol. 49., *Confessio Maior*, fol. 222.). He also calls it a "sacramental union."

However, it should be noted in passing that a great outcry arose in public writings against that synecdoche of Luther as soon as his *Confessio Maior* was published. They cried out that, if a synecdoche is admitted, then it turns the whole phrase, "This is My body," into a figurative expression, for even elementary school children learn that a synecdoche is a figure of speech. Even now there are some who sophistically pretend not to be engaging in logomachy, whether it is said to be synecdoche or metonymy or some other name, as long as a figure of speech is admitted into the phrase, "This is My body."

But it is certain and clear that the question about the individual words in the proposition is one thing, namely, whether they have a proper meaning or a metaphorical or figurative meaning, and there is another question about what kind of predication this is—a predication in those mysteries which do not occur in a natural but in a supernatural and heavenly way. For example, if someone asks whether there is a figure of speech in that phrase, "This Man, Christ, is God," the right response is that both "Man" and "God" retain their proper meanings, without a figure of speech. But if someone asks what kind of predication it is, some call it "unusual." Luther calls it "synecdoche," because those two natures, the divine and the human, are united in one person.

If Arius should exclaim here, "Then we are victorious! For if it is a synecdoche, then the entire phrase is a figure of speech in those words, 'Man is God,' and consequently Christ must not be true and natural God. He is only called that as a form of expression!"—I say, if Arius should say such a thing, all men of sound mind would both understand and call down a curse upon his manifest sophistry. And, in the same way, when Luther disputes about the vocables of the statement, "This is My body," he does not contend that it is a figurative expression, but that the proper meaning of both bread and body must been retained. But when he explains the mode of predication, he says it is "synecdoche," and he says this because the Papists, on account of an identical predication, remove from the Supper the substance of the bread, while the Sacramentarians remove the substance of Christ's body. Luther teaches that, according to the words of institution, both things must be retained, and he shows that it is common, both in Scripture and in common speech, that when two things come together and are united, they are counted as one, and the predications are made as of one thing.

He calls this mode of predication "synecdoche," which, in the Lord's Supper, is no different than what Irenaeus says, that the Eucharist is made up of two things, one earthly and the other heavenly, and that with those things which are seen—bread and wine—the body and blood of Christ are truly and substantially (though invisibly) present and offered. Thus Luther's synecdoche does not in any way defend the figurative expression used by the Zwinglians; it skillfully and clearly explains the true understanding. But if anyone wants to be more contentious and attack these arguments about the mode of predication, we shall answer him with the words of Hilary, who says this about the Sacrament: "In the things of God, we must not speak in a human or worldly sense, nor should the perversity of a foreign and ungodly understanding be twisted out of the soundness of the heavenly sayings by means of violence and shameless predication."

In my judgment, this comparison of propositions can be usefully employed in this way in order to clarify this controversy, for many idle questions are thus cut short, many false accusations are refuted, and the true sources concerning modes of speaking are demonstrated, of which more will be said below.

VI. The physical eating of the bread and the twofold eating of the body of Christ in the Supper: sacramental and spiritual.

Many venomous calumnies have been strewn about since this controversy was first stirred up, and they are still being disseminated against those churches which confess the true presence of the body and blood of Christ in the Supper, as if they taught some kind of Capernaitic butchering of the body of Christ and a Scythian gulping down of the gore of His veins. In addition, the Zwinglians disturb the consciences of many with their insidious equivocation concerning the bodily eating. For human reason neither knows nor understands any other eating than that crass and natural one, like an ox eating hay. There can be no doubt, therefore, that much light will be shed on this subject if a simple distinction is shown to exist among the kinds of eating which occur in this Supper—that is, as far as we are able to know and understand anything in these mysteries from the Word of God. There is no need to go searching for strange arguments, for the very brevity and simplicity of the institution clearly and definitively demonstrates this doctrine for us.

It is certain, then, that the bread is eaten in the Supper. For Paul says, "As often as you eat this bread, etc." (1 Corinthians 11:26).

Furthermore, it is also certain that not only bread is eaten in the Supper. For Christ says of that which is received and eaten, "This is My body." Therefore, the body of Christ is also eaten in the Supper, and not only in a spiritual way, for the unworthy also eat. If the words "to eat" in the words of institution only meant to become a partaker by faith, then there would be no need for the mouth to receive anything in the Supper, but the sense would be, "Take and eat," that is, only hear, ponder, and believe, as the people in Luke 8 "take" the Word of God. But in the Supper, Christ defined the manner of taking in this way: "Take and eat." If only a spiritual eating were to be understood here, then no one could eat judgment upon himself. Therefore, it is clear that there are three kinds of eating in the Supper.

First, there is the eating of the bread, which is not incorrectly called a "physical" eating.

Second, there is the "sacramental" eating of the body of Christ, as it is called by ancient usage. Luther calls it a "bodily or oral" (*leiblich/mündtlich*) eating.

Third, there is the spiritual eating of the body of Christ.

We shall speak separately about each of these, using that simplicity which is fitting for the words of institution and which will benefit those who are less educated.

The **physical eating**, then, is well-known and obvious. For it is the eating of a visible thing which can be perceived by the senses, for the purpose of satisfying a natural hunger, and it happens in a natural way, namely, when food is ground with the teeth, chewed in the mouth, and passed through the throat into the stomach, where it is converted into a liquid, then changed into a nutrient in the liver, the excess portion being expelled into the sewer, etc. Indeed, apart from the fact that common sense and experience convince us of this, the ancient writers also testify that the substance of the bread is eaten in the Eucharist in this way. Origen, commenting on Matthew 15: "The consecrated bread, as pertains to the material, goes down into the stomach and is then expelled into the sewer." Augustine, book 3 of *De Trinitate*, ch. 10: "The bread made for this purpose is consumed in receiving the Sacrament. Now, one may ask whether the body of Christ is also eaten in the Supper in this manner, and since reason neither knows nor understands any other kind of eating, the Capernaites imagined that Christ would cut off bits of His body and give them to be eaten, as cow flesh tends to be eaten after it has been purchased in the market and cooked. But they are sharply rebuked by Christ." Augustine often refutes that

Scythian idea. Luther also states often and in many places his own understanding of the bodily eating in this way, that he does not understand a Capernaitic butchering of the body of Christ.

Therefore, since the body of Christ is eaten in the Supper, but not in a physical, Capernaitic way, the Zwinglians loudly prattle that it is only a spiritual eating, that the soul, applying to itself the benefits of Christ which He merited by the giving of His body, spiritually eats the body of Christ in this way. But Paul expressly says that the unworthy, who do not eat spiritually, become guilty of the body of the Lord by eating that bread which bears that divine designation (*nominationem Dei,* as Irenaeus says), "This is My body." Nor is it metonymy, as if only the external sign were being eaten, for the words of institution expressly and clearly say, "That which you take and eat with your mouth—this is My body." Therefore, we rightly and necessarily acknowledge and believe that, in the Supper, there is also a sacramental eating of the body of Christ in addition to the spiritual eating.

However, it is difficult to provide for this sort of eating a description as obvious as the one provided for the physical eating, for the sacramental union of the body with the bread is a mystery which is incomprehensible to us in this life. But as much as has been given to us to know from the Word of God about this eating here in this darkness of ours, seeing in a mirror dimly, I shall note from the descriptions of those who have explained this question more carefully.

"Therefore, when the flesh of Christ is eaten in the Sacrament, it is not received visibly, nor according to our senses. It is not mutilated. It is not ground with the teeth. It is not dissolved, or digested, or used up. It is not changed into flesh and blood in the manner of other foods." These are the words of Luther concerning this saying; namely, that it is not a physical eating which is done in a natural way, as mentioned above. For "death shall no longer have mastery over Him." Likewise, "He will not see corruption" (Acts 2).

So Chrysostom says in *De Encaeniis*, "Surely it does not go into the sewer as other food, does it? Far be it!" And Paschasius refutes the opposite conclusion in a lengthy oration.

But this sacramental eating of the body of Christ is not to be divorced entirely from the physical eating of the bread, for the words of institution combine both things. He took bread, gave thanks, broke it, and said, "Take, eat; this is My body." Therefore, the mouth, as it receives the bread in the Supper, does not eat common bread, as Irenaeus says, but that bread with which the body of Christ, which was given for us, is truly and substantially present and offered to those who eat. But the mouth does not eat the body of Christ in a physical way (as happens with the chewing, swallowing, and digesting of the bread), for the union or presence is not physical, and yet the mouth truly eats the body of Christ. For the Son of God affirms this, and the union or presence of the body and blood of Christ with the bread and wine, though not physical, is also not figurative or fictional, but real, yet not in a natural way, but in a supernatural and heavenly way. This is a description of sacramental eating.

Therefore, it must be believed most simply according to the words of institution that, in the reception of the Sacrament, those who eat and drink the body and blood of Christ, which are truly and substantially present and offered to the mouth with both the bread and the wine, receive it in such a way that, by means of this reception, the body and blood of the Lord are joined, not only to the soul by faith, but also to the bodies of those who eat, not only by efficacy, but by the very substance, in a way which is known only to Him who is the Author of this tremendous mystery, while incomprehensible and ineffable to us; and that this is done, not to nourish our bodies as the food goes down into the stomach, but to be a heavenly and spiritual nourishment for believers to eternal life, while it leads to judgment for the unworthy. I consider this to be the simplest way to put these things, for antiquity also spoke in this way, as we shall demonstrate below. For the union or presence of the body of Christ with the bread, and of His blood with the wine, is not physical, but supernatural and heavenly, by the sole power and authority of the word of Christ, who instituted this Sacrament. Therefore, it can be profitably believed, but it cannot be understood and comprehended, and it should by no means be investigated. This, too, is a description of sacramental eating. But Augustine says, *De bono perseverantiae*, ch. 14, "That which has been revealed should by no means be denied simply because that which has been hidden cannot be understood." And Chrysostom says in Homily 45 on John, "When the question arises how anything is done, unbelief arises at the same time, etc."

The **spiritual eating** is of Christ, who is God and man, and of all the benefits which He merited by the giving of His body and by the shedding of His blood, the application of which is through faith, for eternal life and salvation. For those who have placed all their trust in the death and resurrection of Christ are said to feed on His flesh and blood spiritually for eternal life. Yes, this spiritual eating takes place also apart from the use of the Supper, by faith alone, through the word (John 6). But in the Lord's Supper, which requires the external elements and the public proclamation of the death of Christ in the congregation of the faithful, the spiritual eating has this peculiar property, as Luther said, that, although the mouth and tongue neither sense nor understand it, they are receiving something else besides bread and wine. Faith believes that, by means of this reception, Christ applies His benefits to you, for based on the words of institution, it considers with a grateful mind the immense benefit of the Son of God, that He not only joins us to Himself by His Spirit, but that He also intimately joins Himself to us by truly offering us His precious body and blood, so that, by that flesh which was given for the life of the world, now shared with us, we may have life remaining in us, we may be one with Him, bone of His bones and flesh of His flesh, and thus we may have the most certain pledge of our salvation, that our miserable, little bodies may also be admitted into His communion. In sum, sacramental eating pertains to that which is offered together with the bread and wine to those who eat and drink in the Supper. But spiritual eating teaches how it is received by true faith to salvation and eternal life, lest the sacramental eating lead to judgment.

Perhaps below there will be a place for saying more about this spiritual eating in the Supper. Here I merely wanted to explain in the simplest way possible the distinction between the kinds of eating in the Supper, which is necessary for clarifying many disputes.

VII. Concerning the purpose, benefit, and usefulness of the true and substantial (as Bucer says in his Retractationes*) presence, distribution, and reception of the body and blood of Christ in the Supper.*

Throughout this discussion, the Zwinglians, with endless repetitions, emphasize a faith which believes that the bodily presence of Christ in the Supper is neither important nor useful for salvation, that we either acquire salvation more abundantly beforehand through spiritual eating, or that we can obtain it more easily thereby. And therefore, they teach that consciences should not be burdened with a dogma that is so difficult and (as they call it) "absurd," or certainly that the position of those who remove the substantial presence and distribution of the body and blood of Christ from the Supper should not be so harshly condemned.

We will have to say more about this objection later in our refutation of arguments. For now, we shall only briefly note the doctrine about the benefit and usefulness of the true presence and distribution of the body and blood of Christ in the Supper.

Luther rightly and truly answers that, even if nothing but the bare command in the institution had been given, without any mention of the benefit and usefulness, we should not for that reason depart from the clear and manifest words of Christ. But we must grant the Son of God this honor, that He has instituted nothing in the Gospel that would be either useless or harmful to our salvation. And the usefulness is sufficiently great that in this way every high thing that exalts itself against the knowledge of God is cast down, and every thought is taken into captivity to the obedience of Christ (cf. 2 Cor. 10). Likewise, he says that the obedience of our faith is proved in this way, if it believes what Christ says and does what He commands, even if we knew nothing at all about its benefit from the Word of God.

But the fact is that very clear testimonies have been given to us about its benefit and usefulness. For if anyone eats unworthily, he becomes guilty of the body and blood of the Lord and eats judgment on himself, because he does not discern the body of the Lord. Therefore, whoever does discern and eats worthily, he eats salvation for himself, though not by merely doing the work. He receives it with faith. Scripture does not only say these things in general, but it expressly mentions and enumerates what and how great are the advantages that come to us from that presence and reception of the body and blood of Christ, if we eat worthily. Indeed, we must be careful to consider this doctrine often and always to keep it before our eyes, for thus we shall more correctly understand those things which are disputed concerning the substance of the Lord's Supper. We shall love the true understanding more and defend it more diligently, and we shall not allow it to be cast away from ourselves lightly, as many do who think that no great harm is done if that presence is utterly removed from the Lord's Supper.

In my opinion, however, the matter will be simplest if we do not accumulate testimonies that are foreign to the matter at hand, but confine ourselves to the terms used in the institution, for the institution embraces the entire doctrine, not only about the presence of the substance of the body and blood of Christ, but also about the purpose, benefit, and usefulness of that presence. And all of that can be more easily retained—not to mention being better understood—if it is set forth with the very words of institution.

Therefore, the first usefulness is commonly said to be the strengthening of faith. This is stated thus in the words of institution: "This do in remembrance of Me." Indeed, the words are very significant if the Scriptural phrase is considered. For just as the loss of faith is called "forgetting" (2 Peter 1), so the unfeigned "remembering" is a real description of a living and growing faith. Second Tim. 2: "Remember that Christ rose again from the dead." And the word "remembrance" (ἀναμνήσεως) emphasizes something very important, for it means to recall into memory those things which, either through forgetfulness or through one's own fault, have begun to disappear from the mind, as in Mark 14. When the rooster crowed, Peter was reminded (ἀνεμνήσθη) of the word of Christ, which he had previously not taken very seriously, and therefore it had disappeared from his mind. And in 2 Tim. 1: "I remind you (ἀναμιμνήσκω σε) to stir up the gift of God which is in you," namely, lest it be extinguished through negligence.

Moreover, every believer experiences, as he sighs under the weight of this corruptible flesh, how manifold is the infirmity of his faith, how faint is his belief, how easily it is shaken by temptations and just barely escapes being driven out, how quickly he is overwhelmed by the thorns of this world, and almost overcome by security, so that he is not ardent in meditation, trust, invocation, and thanksgiving. And since this wretched infirmity of the wounded and despoiled nature in His believers was not unknown to Christ the true Samaritan, He instituted various remedies for raising it up. For He says concerning the ministry of the word in John 14, "The Holy Spirit will bring to your remembrance (ὑπομνήσει) all things which I have said to you." And concerning meditation on the word, David says in Psalm 103, "Forget not, O my soul!" It says the same thing throughout Psalm 119.

But there is no more efficacious antidote against the forgetfulness of which Peter speaks than what the Son of God instituted in the Supper: "Take, eat; this is My body. Drink; this is My blood. This do in remembrance of Me (εἰς τὴν ἐμὴν ἀνάμνησιν)." For if true faith does not lay hold as firmly as it is laid hold of by Christ (Phi. 3), what more effective way could there be to create, nourish, and preserve a true and unfeigned remembrance of Christ than when He lays hold of believers through the natural participation (as the ancients say) in His own body and blood in the Supper? For that is a life-giving flesh, to which the divinity is conjoined by personal union. If this flesh is truly and substantially offered to us in the Supper, will not our faith have the best and most powerful antidote against temptations, security, and any occasion for forgetting? This consideration stirs up the minds of men to true reverence of this most sacred mystery, so that they may use it more frequently, with true humility, trust, and thanksgiving.

Second. The words of institution say, "This cup is the New Testament in My blood, etc." Now, the New Testament consists of the forgiveness of sins, God's grace, adoption, salvation, and eternal life (Jer. 31, Heb. 8). These things are offered to all men in general in the preaching of the Gospel. But here the Son of God says to each one individually, "Take, drink; this cup is the New Testament in My blood." Therefore, He testifies that He is giving and applying to you all the benefits which He acquired by the shedding of His blood. And what could be a more certain and a more precious seal or pledge of this assertion and application than that He holds out to be received that very blood by which the New Testament was sealed, which is truly and substantially present?

We should ponder now how great is the usefulness of that presence and distribution which we are defending from the Word of God. Alas! How often we violate and transgress that covenant of a good conscience which God initiated with us in Baptism! But the Son of God cries out in His Supper, "As often as you wish, take!

Eat! This cup is the New Testament!" Therefore, we are received again into that covenant and are strengthened in our confidence in it. Now, what sweeter and surer consolation could there be for terrified consciences, so that they do not doubt that they are truly included in that new covenant before God, than the fact that Christ has said, "That which you take and drink is My very blood by which the New Testament was sealed, for it was shed for you for the forgiveness of sins. That which you take is My body, which is given for you." This pledge and seal of the body and blood, which are truly and substantially present and offered to us, we set against all temptations and doubts by a true faith. Now, who in his right mind will claim that such a great treasure of the true presence of the body and blood of Christ is taken away from the Supper and from us?

Third. These words of institution are strongly emphasized, "This is My body, which is given for you." Paul complains of that misery which all the godly experience daily, that in our flesh nothing good dwells, but only the law of sin, rebelling against the law of the mind and taking us captive, so that what we do not want, that we also do, etc. Therefore Christ says, "Take and eat; this is My body." For as Cyril said, "For the flesh of the Savior, joined with the Word of God, which is by nature life, has become life-giving. When we eat it, we have life in ourselves, for we have been joined to that which has become life, so that those members which are flesh of Adam's flesh and bone of his bones, may thus be put to death more and more, that we may be made members of Christ, of His flesh and of His bones, as the Scripture says, when, as shoots grafted into the substance of Him, we draw life from Him, like branches from a vine."

We should ponder these things with pious meditation as we use the Supper. Our body is a body of sin. Therefore, the Son of God says, "Take and eat; this is My body." I am speaking briefly about the greatest things on which we should piously meditate. The Zwinglians cry out that the most pure substance of Christ's flesh would be polluted by our filth, if it were "mingled with us," as Chrysostom and Cyril say.

But we gratefully acknowledge and celebrate this immense kindness of God's Son, that He did not scorn to join His most holy body and His most pure blood with this wretched flesh of ours, polluted in so many ways, in order that, having grafted us into Himself, He might vivify, carry, and guide us. Moreover, we believe that He is not polluted by us, just as the rays of the sun are not polluted by dirt, etc.

Fourth. From this point, Irenaeus makes a delightful argument for the future immortality and glorification of our bodies. For however much our bodies are miserable and subject to death and infinite calamities, yet "since they are nourished by the body and blood of Christ," as he says, "it necessarily follows that they cannot entirely perish, nor can they forever be exposed to those miseries which they experience in this life, but must be admitted into the communion of life, glory, and incorruptibility." The passages of Irenaeus are well-known. Cyril says this: "The nature of this corruptible body could not otherwise pass to incorruptibility and life, unless the body of natural life had been joined to it." This sweet consolation is entirely removed if the true presence and distribution of the body and blood of Christ in the Supper are denied. The very ancient writer Justin says this: "By that food (namely, the body and blood of Christ) our flesh and blood are nourished by a change (κατὰ μεταβολήν)," that is, not by digestion, as happens with other foods, but because that Eucharistic food changes the mortality of our bodies into its own nature; namely, immortality, life, and glory. Luther takes that saying of Justin and explains it with this crude analogy: "If a sheep had such a nature that, once eaten by a wolf, it changed the wolf's ferocity into sheep-like tameness, so the food of the body of Christ is not changed into our blood, but it changes us into itself."

Finally, it is rightly said that this communion is a bond of mutual love and fellowship. Just as there is one bread, so we who are many are one body. But just as the Eucharist consists of two things, an earthly and a heavenly, so this communion is a bond of mutual love in two ways.

First, it is the bond of mutual love by signification. As Augustine says in his Tractate 26 on John: "Christ committed His body and blood to those things which are rendered into one thing from many things. For bread is made and consists of many grains. Wine flows into one drink from many grapes. Therefore, Christ intends for us to understand the affinity of His body and of His members, that is, the Holy Church."

Second, it is the bond of mutual love also by efficacy. For Christ, who is truly and substantially present with His body and blood and is distributed and received in the Supper, effectively works this, that since the Head itself is in us, we, in turn, are members one of the other (Eph. 4). And in 1 Cor. 12: "We have all been made to drink into one Spirit."

These things are certainly and manifestly gathered from the words of institution. And thus it is evident that this doctrine of the benefit and usefulness of the true presence and distribution of the body and blood of Christ in the Supper is thoroughly delightful and vitally important, for it also shows how and with what kind of faith it is to be approached. For he who eats unworthily, without repentance and faith, becomes guilty of the body and blood of the Lord and eats judgment on himself, as we shall say below.

But this doctrine will be better understood when consciences, in using this Sacrament, experience the sweet consolation and efficacy of the Son of God from the true and serious meditation on this doctrine, which is set forth in the very words of institution for the purpose that, in using the Supper, it should ever be kept in sight.

From these things it is now clear how many treasures are stolen from us by those who attempt to remove the true presence of

Christ's body and blood from the Supper. And when we consider these causes carefully, in the fear of God, from the very words of institution, then we will also both hold more tenaciously to the true understanding and we will more ardently detest the Zwinglian perversions.

VIII. In which passages of Scripture the right faith concerning the Lord's Supper is to be sought.

Yes, even these things which we have mentioned up until now pertain to the simple and bare explanation of that doctrine which believes and confesses the true and "real" (as Bucer speaks in his *Retractationes*) presence of the body and blood of the Lord in the Supper. But faith does not rest on human assertions; it must be built upon the foundation of the Prophets and Apostles, for there is a great difference between assurance (πληροφορίαν) and blind belief (τύφλωσιν). Assurance is derived from the firm and clear foundations of God's Word; but blind belief is presumed on the basis of private imaginations, by a certain obstinacy and a desire to make assertions. Therefore, the firm and solid foundations of our understanding must be demonstrated in the Word of God, so that, having been reinforced by these foundations against all arguments, however plausible, consciences may be able to rest safely and firmly on the true understanding. Moreover, just as each article of the faith has its own proper seat (*sedes*), as it were, in certain firm passages of Scripture, from whence the true and genuine understanding of those things is to be sought, so in this controversy the chief consideration should be this: Which testimonies of Scripture deal with the particular topic of the doctrine of the Lord's Supper? Where are its true foundations to be sought?

Nor should this recollection be considered a waste of time, for it is well-known how the "craftiness of deceitful plotting" (μεθοδεία τῆς πλάνης, as Paul calls it) first ushered in the error of the Sacramentarians and how it is still maintained. They deal with the passages concerning the institution of circumcision, and of the Paschal lamb, concerning the sacrifice of the red heifer, and concerning the ark of the covenant. Likewise, they cite the case of Ahijah giving Jeroboam ten pieces of his garment, etc. And from these and similar passages, they first establish what they want to believe and conclude about the Lord's Supper. Afterwards, a certain place is also given to the words of institution. I shall recite in their own words their reason for doing so. This is what Zwingli says: "We agree on the principal matter" (namely, about the absence of the body of Christ in the Supper), "but with the inexperienced, the words of institution seem to be a hindrance both to us and others. Each one now makes some attempt," namely, to interpret the words of institution in such a way that they do not conflict with the presumed opinion previously given.

He goes on, "Likewise, we treat these words (This is My body; this is My blood), one person one way, another person another way, in order to make it simple enough for the little ones who are still licking the outer shell of the words and do not penetrate to the kernel." Therefore, they openly admit that they have not learned their understanding of the Lord's Supper from the words of institution, but as Hilary says, "They have brought their own understanding to the words of the Supper, which they had presumed to be the understanding even before reading them." And from here this method is observed in the writings of all the Zwinglians, that among those arguments which they accumulate to establish and confirm their own understanding of the Lord's Supper, these words ("This is My body"; "This is My blood") do not have their proper place, but are used in refutation, where those things which seem to be opposed to the established understanding are normally recited and explained. There, at length, with great effort, as Zwingli says, these words resound, "This is My body, etc." I am reciting these things so that it may be carefully considered that the starting points in this controversy, as it has been rightly and skillfully arranged, are more than half of the whole, as they say. Namely, that we may understand what the true beginnings are, what the progression and the goals have been.

However, beyond all controversy it is absolutely certain that the right faith about the Lord's Supper has its proper place and its proper seat (*sedes*) in the words of institution. Therefore, here is where the true foundations must be sought, if we wish to know with certainty what we are to conclude and believe about this Sacrament. To this place as to the true fountains we must return, if any doubts or disputations about this Sacrament arise, not only from the notions that come from reason, but also from other passages of Scripture. Indeed, the Son of God Himself gives us an example of this method. For when the Pharisees stirred up an argument about dissolving marriage and, with a plausible appearance, offered, not their own ideas, but a passage from Deuteronomy about the certificate of divorce, Christ does not want the seat and proof of the argument about divorce to be located in that passage from Deuteronomy about the certificate of divorce. No, He calls the whole controversy back to the fountains and foundations of the institution. "Have you not read that the One who made man from the beginning made them and said, 'For this reason a man will leave, etc.?'"

So, too, when Paul was consulted about certain disagreements which had begun to arise in the Corinthian church about the Lord's Supper, he calls the whole matter of right faith and the true use back to that first institution, as they had it described for them by the Evangelists, whose words he also religiously cites. Indeed, he affirms that when he received his Gospel, not from a man, but through revelation of Jesus Christ, he also received the doctrine about the Lord's Supper which he was to set forth and pass on with the same words as the Evangelists used in their description of the institution. He says, "I received from the Lord," not, of course, as the Lord reclined at the table in the upper room in Jerusalem, but from the Lord sitting at the right hand of the eternal Father.

Therefore, it is absolutely certain that the true foundations of the doctrine of the Lord's Supper are to be sought, drawn, and learned from the institution itself. Indeed, it must be done in this way so that the true and genuine understanding of this Sacrament may be deduced from those words, understood properly and without sophistry, according to the native character of the words. For insolent tricksters should not be permitted the license to overturn the proper and native understanding of the words of institution through an understanding so astutely devised and concocted that it seems to agree somehow with certain other passages of Scripture. For this is how Pelagius long ago used to toy with that passage in Romans 5 which he understood to be only about imitation: that many people are corrupted by the examples of vices, as by a contagion. He was easily able to produce many testimonies and examples of this opinion of his from other passages of Scripture, and it was not difficult for him somehow to accommodate the text of Romans 5 to that opinion. And then he exclaims that the analogy of faith must be used in the interpretation of Scripture, and that the "fewer" passages (as Tertullian says) must be explained according to the "many" (*pauciora exponenda secundum plura*).

But the distinction is clear and necessary. In some passages of Scripture, the articles of faith are set forth with figurative language or with obscure words. In those passages, the method of interpretation is valid of which Augustine speaks in book 2, *De doctrina Christiana*, namely, "Let a certain understanding be reached which is in agreement with other clearer passages. And when the words of a more obscure passage can be accommodated somehow to that understanding, then the interpretation is good." But in some passages, the dogmas or articles of faith are founded and explained as in a proper seat. Surely the true and native understanding of those dogmas should be entirely drawn from those passages, properly and without sophistry, being understood according to the character of the words. If a foreign interpretation in admitted in those passages, in addition to the literal sense—an interpretation that has been derived from some other passages of Scripture—then nothing will be left of the entire Scripture. Therefore, since the proper place of the doctrine concerning the Lord's Supper is in the words of institution, it is clear from the arguments we have made why the right faith about the Lord's Supper must be derived from those words; namely, so that we do not conceive any opinion for ourselves from a different place and then bend the words of institution to that opinion. Instead, we should follow the lovely rule of Hilary, book 1, *De Trinitate*: "That reader is best who awaits the understanding of the sayings from the sayings themselves rather than imposing his understanding on them; who reports, not imports, the understanding; who does not force the sayings to seem to contain that which he presumed, before reading, to be the proper understanding."

This is why I have noted these things somewhat more thoroughly. For when our thoughts turn to that preposterous method which is customary to the Zwinglians, we experience how clever they seem, how they flatter themselves with their own acumen. Therefore, let us always imagine that the furious voice of Christ is resounding in our ears and minds, the voice with which He repressed the Pharisees in a similar discussion: "Have you not read?" For He who first instituted the Sacrament has said, "This is My body. This is My blood."

IX. *The status of this controversy.*

Fallacy, as they call it in the schools with regard to many inquiries, gives rise to great disturbances in all matters. But in this controversy especially, consciences are easily disturbed when a forest of various questions and foreign arguments is added into it. Therefore, it is useful rightly to establish and often to examine the "title," if I may call it so, of this discussion, lest we be displaced from the true status by means of foreign questions.

Therefore, the controversy between the Zwinglians and us is not about the transubstantiation of the bread into the body of Christ, nor about the local inclusion of the body of Christ in the bread, nor about the immense and infinite ubiquity of the body of Christ, nor about the Capernaitic butchering of the flesh of Christ, nor even about the adoration of the elements of bread and wine. Nor is it disputed what the benefit and usefulness is of spiritual eating. For we explain clearly and expressly what spiritual eating is, and we affirm that those who only eat sacramentally and not also spiritually eat judgment on themselves and are made guilty of the body and blood of the Lord. But this is the status of the controversy: It is certain that something is present in the Lord's Supper; that Christ, by the hand of the minister, offers or distributes something; and that He commands us to take something. Indeed, when He says, "Eat, drink," He is showing us how we should take it; namely, by receiving something with the mouth. The question is, "What is that which is present in the Lord's Super, which is offered to those who eat and drink, which we take and receive with the mouth?" Here the senses of sight, touch, and taste understand that it is bread and wine. The Evangelists also say that Christ "took bread, broke it, and gave it to His disciples." They similarly refer to the "fruit of the vine" in the cup. And Paul says, "The bread which we break." Likewise, "Whoever eats this bread."

But the question is, is it only bread, whether common and vulgar, or merely consecrated like the loaves of showbread? Here we must not deal with conjectures or with guesses. We seek firm and solid foundations.

The Truth Itself responds: "This—which is present with the bread in the Eucharist, which is offered to those who eat and drink, which you take and eat—is My body, which is given for you. As for what is given to you with the wine in the cup, which you take and drink: This is My blood, etc." If these words of the Son of God are to be understood in their genuine and simple sense, which is found in the native, customary, grammatical, and certain meaning of the words themselves, then the matter is perfectly clear. That body which was given for us, and that blood by the shedding of which the New Testament was sealed, are present in the Supper with the bread and wine and are offered to those who eat and drink.

The entire focus, then, is on this: that it may be demonstrated that we do not have any reasons from the Word of God which are sufficiently serious, firm, or certain to cause us to depart from the well-known, customary, and perspicuous words. On the contrary, we have perspicuous, firm, and certain testimonies in the declarations which the Holy Spirit Himself has provided in the Scripture in this matter. That sense must be embraced and retained which the proper, customary, and certain meaning of the words furnishes. Once this has been established, the entire adjudication of this controversy will be resolved, and the reason for our faith, the confession of which we mentioned and explained above, will be rendered true, firm, and sufficient. And then we shall also safely be able to rest in that most fundamental simplicity, even if we are not able to disentangle all the verbal trickery of our adversaries or settle all their questions.

For it is observable that, after Paul had passed on to Timothy the whole corpus of heavenly doctrine, in the end he gave him two precepts. If he wanted to guard the deposit faithfully, he was to beware, first, lest he be moved away from the simplicity of the faith through attractive antitheses, which can seem quite scholarly. Second, he was to beware, lest he allow his faith to be disturbed by clever words and inextricable questions. The passages include 1 Timothy 6: "O Timothy, guard the deposit, avoiding profane novelties of words and the contradictions of knowledge falsely named. By professing it, some have fallen away concerning the faith." Likewise: "Those who are obsessed with questions know nothing and have been deprived of the truth." Also 2 Timothy 2, Titus 3, etc.

The summary of the Zwinglians' opinion should also be added here, to make the matter clearer. Some say that it is only a sign. As bread is broken, so was the body broken that was given for us. Others say that it is only a symbol. As bread nourishes the body, so Christ is the food for the soul. Now practically all cry out that the benefits, merits, righteousness, fellowship, etc., of the body of Christ, which was given for us, and of the blood of Christ, which was shed for us, are offered and distributed in the Eucharist. But they say that the substance itself of the body and blood of Christ is not present in the Supper, but resides in a certain defined place in heaven, so that it cannot be in more than one place at the same time. This is what Calvin says: "As I have said, the body of Christ is distributed in the Supper effectively, not naturally; it is distributed according to power, not according to substance." Peter Martyr says, "I remove from the Eucharist the presence of the body of Christ, whereby He is believed to be in many places at the same time (namely, where the Lord's Supper is celebrated, according to the institution). But if someone understands by 'presence' the perception of faith, whereby we ourselves ascend into heaven and embrace Christ in His majesty with our mind and spirit, with him I agree."

All these men pretend that the efficacy of the body of Christ is present in the Supper and is offered to those who eat and drink, even though His presence is absent. But if the words of Christ ("This is My body, which is given for you; this is My blood, etc.") are taken in their proper sense, which the native and certain meaning of the vocables renders, then the understanding is so manifest that not even our adversaries can deny it; namely, that the body of Christ is present and distributed in the Supper, not only with regard to efficacy, but also with regard to substance. For beyond all controversy, the substance of the body of Christ was given for us, and the substance of His blood was shed for us.

This is the status of the controversy, to which all the arguments, both for confirmation and for refutation, should be directed.

X. The strongest arguments for the position that one should not depart from the character of those words, "This is My body, which is given for you, etc."

Since, then, this whole controversy hinges (as they say) on this status, we must repeat again that reminder which was mentioned at the outset; namely, that it is not an idle or harmless game when clever men play around with the words, "This is My body." For terrifying statements have been added: "He will be guilty of the body and blood of the Lord." Likewise: "Whoever does not discern the body of the Lord eats judgment on himself."

Now, it is certain that such discernment requires knowledge, as we said at the outset. Therefore, it is useful and entirely necessary always to stay focused on the sure and firm foundations of the true understanding by which the mind, instructed and fortified ahead of time against all arguments, no matter how beautiful or plausible they may be, may rest, with Christ's own help, on the simple understanding of the words of Christ. Indeed, those words have been pointed out skillfully and confirmed with abundant eloquence in many of our writings, but especially those of Dr. Luther.

Therefore, I do not wish to say anything new, but only to repeat the things that are old, as they say. But since simpler people are not so easily able to attend to the principal headings and the true thrust of the subject matters in extensive writings, I set out many years ago, with a fair amount of diligence, to note down and collect the chief arguments for why one should not depart from the character of the words of institution. And I experienced that such simplicity was often beneficial in this controversy, both for me and for others who were less educated. In my judgment, the arguments can comfortably be divided into three classes, for the sake of order and instruction.

First should be placed those arguments which are taken from the perpetual analogy which the Holy Spirit commanded to be observed in interpreting those passages where the dogmas or articles of faith are founded.

Second, from the comparison and agreement of those passages in which the doctrine of the Lord's Supper has been described.

Third, from the unanimous confession of the ancient and purer Church; that is, from the testimonies of antiquity.

XI. Arguments from the certain and perpetual analogy of interpretation which the Holy Spirit gave to be observed in those passages where the dogmas about the essence and will of God are properly founded.

Peter says that the Scripture is not of private interpretation, for we are not permitted the kind of license that would allow each one to paste or to affix without danger a peculiar interpretation to those passages where the dogmas are especially presented. But in order that faith may be certain, a certain method has been pointed out in the Scripture itself which is to be followed in explaining such passages. And from there many beautiful arguments are drawn, of which I shall recite only a few which are able to inform the judgment of simpler people.

First

It is nothing new for the impudence of human ingenuity to invent for itself certain absurd and disagreeable things in the passages where the dogmas are presented, on account of which it thinks that it can rightly depart from the clear words of Scripture, thinking that it is great wisdom to be able to elude the clarity of the words by means of some attractive interpretation.

Indeed, Scripture itself mentions several such artificial corruptions in the clearest of words, and the refutations of them have been added by the Holy Spirit Himself, undoubtedly for this reason, to teach a certain rule which should be safely followed in serious controversies of this kind in which the dogmas of the faith are being disputed; namely, that in articles of faith we should not embrace the persuasive expositions of human reason when they depart from the manifest character of the words. Since those examples usefully shed light on this whole controversy, I shall briefly note some of them.

The most elucidating example is in the story of Abraham. God had given him the promise of the Seed (Gen. 12 & 13). But since Abraham was worn out and Sarah was sterile (Gen. 15), he began to philosophize in this way: What if the promise were to be understood concerning an adopted seed? In that case, the promise would still remain true! And yet, he did not take these thoughts at once for an oracle of God, but poured them into God's lap and sought instruction. But God responded, "He who comes from your own body, him you shall have for an heir."

Sarah understood well the import of these words, for there is nothing obscure about them. But since she could not comprehend how it could be, she invented an attractive interpretation by which she did not unreasonably depart, as it seemed to her, from the simple and proper sense of the words of the promise. She said, "Go in to my maidservant, if I may at least be built up from her." Thus departing from the word itself, it seemed to her that she was holding beautifully to the idea behind the promise. Indeed, she did not want to seem to have undertaken this from the depraved arguments of reason. But since, she said, the Lord has closed me up so that I cannot bear children, it must be that there is another understanding of the promise than that which the sound of the words properly implies. But in chapter 17, the Lord provided a clarifying repetition, so that, if anything in the previous words could produce obscurity, He might reveal it and more pointedly declare the simple understanding by means of that repetition, saying, "You shall not call your wife Sarai, but Sarah. And I will bless her and give you a son from her."

But how? The text says, "Abraham laughed and thought in his heart, 'Do You mean that a son will be born to a hundred-year-old man, and that Sarah will give birth at the age of ninety?'" So convinced he was that it could not be.

The promise is also repeated a fourth time in chapter 18—"Surely I will return to you according to the time of life, and Sarah your wife will have a son"—so that they might truly understand from so many repetitions, which were made with the same words, that they were not to depart from the character of the words. But, the text says, "since they were both old and well-advanced in years, and the womanly ways of Sarah had ceased, she secretly laughed."

But since God had shown the true understanding of the promise through multiple repetitions, and since Abraham seemed only to hesitate over how it could be done, God finally brought him to consider His divine omnipotence. For this is what it says: "Why did your wife Sarah laugh, saying, 'Surely I will not really give birth, being an old woman, will I?' Is anything too difficult for God?"

Thus in the example of Abraham, who is the father of the faith, God wanted to teach his posterity by depicting the arguments of human wisdom concerning the interpretation of the dogmas of the faith and, at the same time, show the true path which must be followed in controversies of this sort.

Paul writes something very noteworthy in Romans 4. After Abraham had on several occasions attempted a metaphorical interpretation of the promise, and then understood from so many repetitions of it, which made it clear, by using the same and ever clearer words, that he was not to depart from the character of the vocables, finally, Paul says, "he did not consider his dead body and the dead womb of Sarah, for he did not doubt the promise of God through unbelief, but was strengthened in faith, giving glory to God, knowing full well that, whatever God promised, He was also able to accomplish." The application of this example to the present controversy is clear; it very usefully elucidates many things in these discussions.

A similar example is described in Matthew 22. The Sadducees denied the resurrection of the dead because of the many absurd things they imagined would follow logically from that teaching. But they did not want to seem as if they were measuring those absurdities by the judgment of reason. Instead, they tried to show that the article of the resurrection was in conflict with the very Law of God. For John the Baptist so detested the idea of a man having the wife of a living brother that he did not hesitate to put his own life in danger. Indeed, the Law of God in no way permits one woman to be married to seven living husbands at the same time—and brothers at that! But Christ simply responds, "You are wrong, for you do not know the Scriptures or the power of God. For God has a different manner of resurrection than you can comprehend with your thoughts. They will not marry, nor will they be given in marriage, but they will be like the angels of God, and yet there will be a true resurrection, and it will be to true life."

Therefore, according to the Son of God, this is the analogy of true interpretation. Just because we do not know or comprehend how to understand something does not mean that we should immediately depart from the words in the articles of faith. For God is far more able than we can imagine to bring about the things He has said. And when we say the same thing about the Lord's Supper, we do not do so without an example. No, the very One who said, "This is My body," has given us that instruction and has commanded us to respond to all objections: "You are wrong, because you do not know the Scriptures or the power of God." Thus Paul, in 2 Timothy 2, cites the example of Hymenaeus and Phyletus. Like the Sadducees, they did not dare to deny the many Scripture passages which speak of the resurrection in the clearest words. So they contended that such passages do not actually mean what the words properly say, but should be interpreted figuratively about the spiritual resurrection, namely, that of the inner man which happens in this life. And about that spiritual resurrection they were also able to cite many testimonies from Paul's epistles and preaching. For they did not do as Porphyrius and Julianus did, ridiculing the divinely revealed doctrine with sacrilegious audacity. But they undoubtedly gave plausible reasons why they thought to depart from the character of the words in those passages. For when Paul says, "Their speech spreads like gangrene," he indicates well enough that their reasons were either crass inventions or ignorant fables.

Moreover, he does not want Timothy to be disturbed in refuting a figurative interpretation simply because that interpretation is consistent with many other testimonies of Scripture. He simply says, "Avoid these things, for they go astray concerning the truth."

Also applicable here is the argument the Pharisees were making about marriage in Matthew 19. For they pose the question in such a way that they do not deny or reject those words by which God instituted marriage in the beginning, but pretend that, from those Scripture passages where divorce and divorced women are mentioned, as in Deuteronomy 24, they are taking an interpretation that is somewhat more attractive than the words of institution sound if they are understood properly and rigidly. A fine argument! For this method of interpretation is, in many passages, not only useful, but entirely necessary.

But Christ simply responds, "From the beginning it was not so. Have you not read, etc.?" That is, He brings the whole argument back to the first institution of marriage, and from there He wants the interpretation of other sayings to be taken. But He in no way means to concede thereby that the manifest words of institution should be turned away from their proper sense on account of other passages which seem, on the surface, to be in conflict.

But that simplicity of response was not yet satisfactory to the disciples themselves, for Mark writes that they asked Him about the same matter again in the house, and Matthew says that the question was, "Is it expedient?" But Christ merely repeats the meaning of the institution, that "what God has joined together, man should not separate. Therefore, whoever divorces his wife commits adultery, etc."

The application of the examples to the present controversy is evident. For, by His own deed, Christ has prescribed the rule for us, telling us what we should do and what pattern we should safely follow in a similar case and against a similar argument. I have recounted these things so that by the examples it may become obvious that it is not a new trick to employ clever interpretations in order to elude the passages in which God has clearly revealed His will. But the refutations that have been added in the Scripture with such great care by the Holy Spirit Himself usefully and quite splendidly illuminate the path that we must either avoid or follow in this present controversy.

Second

There are undoubtedly many figures of speech used in Scripture. This, too, is certain, that not all things are wrapped under the veils of figures; many things have been openly explained with proper words. Now, if such a license were granted, giving one person the freedom, if it seemed best to him, to depart from the words in some passage, through some clever interpretation, or, giving another person the freedom to retain the character of the words in the very same passage, then all the articles of faith could easily be eluded and undermined. Therefore, there must necessarily be a certain rule for determining in which passages figures of speech are to be admitted and which passages should properly be taken literally, just as the words sound, so that the conscience may safely be able to rest on the revealed understanding. Indeed, Augustine gives us that very canon in some of his own words (Book 3, ch. 10 & 16, *De Doctrina Christiana*). But I want to cite the words of Dr. Philip Melanchthon, which are extremely illustrative.

"The ancients clearly affirm that the body of Christ is present in the Supper, and I cannot find any decent reason why we should depart from that understanding. It can happen that another opinion which is more agreeable to human reason deludes an idle spirit, especially an opinion that is equipped and endowed with skillfully reasoned arguments. But what will happen in times of testing? When the conscience wonders what reason it has to disagree with the received understanding in the Church, then those words, 'This is My body,' will be like lightning bolts. What will the terrified mind set against these words? With what Scriptures, with what Word of God will it fortify itself and persuade itself that here the words have to be interpreted metaphorically? Those who so easily sow novel dogmas do not seem sufficiently experienced with these struggles—men who so delight in their own cleverness that they marvel more at their cunningly devised reasons than at the words of Scripture. I, for one, know how easily those reasons which disagree with Scripture are driven out of our hands in times of testing, no matter how plausible they seemed before.

"It happens in the present controversy more than in others that the universal Church and the whole empire are threatened with a horrible change. Who can bear the conscience of such a great scandal without the clear and certain testimony of Scripture? Therefore, I follow the understanding of the ancient Church, which affirms that the body of Christ is present in the Supper, and I judge that this understanding has the testimony of Scripture. For I do not find a good reason why, with the term 'body' in the words of the Supper, only a sign of an absent body must be understood. For although the language of Holy Scripture is full of every kind of figurative expression, there is a very great difference between narrations of events and between divine ordinances or dogmas about the nature and will of God. In narrations, occurrences among men are related in which a series of acts, subject to our senses, forces us to interpret figuratively the things that are spoken absurdly. If we try to do the same thing in the commandments or dogmas which speak of the nature and will of God, learned men can easily imagine what will happen. In this case, when the absurdity conflicts with other clearer passages of Scripture or with articles of faith, it must be corrected with the help of figurative language. But if it merely conflicts with reason, not with the Scriptures, then it is best to prefer the Word of God over the judgment of reason. For there must necessarily be a certain understanding of those passages from which the dogmas or articles are drawn. If we are permitted to interpret these in any which way, then all things will be subject to distortion.

"Likewise, no passage of Scripture can be cited which testifies that Christ is not present in the Supper or which forces the words of the Supper to be interpreted allegorically. Nor does the use of the ancient Church force those words to be interpreted allegorically; only the absurdity which conflicts with the judgment of reason is at odds with those words. This is not a sufficiently good reason for us to depart from the words. If we allow ourselves to be drawn away from the Scriptures by this kind of absurdity, we will have no protection in any temptation.

"Similarly, those geometric and physical speculations stir up great tumult, both in an empty mind and in the one that has become accustomed to seeking the reasoning behind the doctrine of religion. In fact, all of us who are even a little bit studious do this. But we must return to the Scriptures. And since I find there no testimony that denies that the body of Christ is present in the Supper or that interprets the words of the Supper differently than they sound, I have no sufficiently good reason to teach a new understanding, especially one that stirs up so many scandals, which cannot be endured, as I know very well, unless we have firm and certain testimonies of Scripture."

These are the words of Philip in which this useful and necessary distinction is demonstrated, namely, that there are many difficult passages in Scripture which are rather obscure, due either to the stories or the grammar. In such passages, diverse and dissimilar interpretations do not in any way impede the soundness of faith, as Augustine says in the first book of *De Doctrina Christiana.* "When it comes to interpretation, if anyone offers an opinion that is useful for fostering love, without claiming that the person whom he has read is proven to have understood correctly in that passage, he does not wickedly go astray, nor is he at all guilty of deception." But there is a clear and necessary distinction between those obscurities by which pride is cleansed, as Augustine says elsewhere, and between those passages of Scripture on which the dogmas or articles of faith are founded as in their proper seat. For the dogmas themselves, whether of commandments or of articles of faith, which speak of the nature or will of God, have been presented in Holy Scripture, not obscurely or ambiguously, but clearly, with well-known and manifest words, as Augustine has also noted in book 2, ch. 9 of *De Doctrina Christiana.* "In these matters which have been clearly revealed in Scripture, all those things are found which embrace faith and moral living." For as Peter says, how could the Scripture shine on our darkness and on the dense fog of our mind if the Scripture itself, by its own obscurity or ambiguity in those passages where God reveals His will, rendered the darkness of our mind darker still?

Therefore, in such passages, only one, sure understanding must be sought, and that not from elsewhere; it must be drawn from the context and from the character of the words. But it is clear that no sure understanding can be drawn from the words of institution if one departs from the character of the words, based on the dissenting diversity of interpretations which are held among the Zwinglians.

Third

The following observation is also useful for demonstrating the preceding rule, namely, how zealously the Son of God observed that canon, lest some bit of obscurity remain in the dogmas which might disturb men's consciences. For, after He had said something more obscurely in the parables, He would "explain all things" (Mark 4) to His disciples when they asked, and often when they did not ask. Indeed, He often presented the dogmas in figurative language, as in John 3, concerning regeneration; John 4, concerning the Holy Spirit and eternal life; John 6, concerning the application of the remission of sins; Matthew 16, concerning fleeing from false doctrine. But when He wanted something to be understood differently than the words sounded, lest the hearers be buffeted by some metaphorical wind, He permitted them at first to speculate in their private thoughts about the sense, so that He might thus have occasion to explain the figurative language with well-known, proper, and perspicuous words, lest any ambiguity remain in those passages which He wanted to be well-known to all, both wise and unwise.

Thus Nicodemus does not at first accept and understand rebirth differently than the words sound in their proper and usual meaning, just as the Samaritan woman understands the water, the crowds the eating of Christ's flesh, and the Apostles the yeast. But since Christ wants those words to be interpreted metaphorically, He Himself first reveals that the words are not to be understood as they sound. Then He teaches the meaning, and that not with obscure or ambiguous words, but with well-known and clear words He reveals what He wants to be understood figuratively with rebirth, water, food, yeast, etc.

So the rule remains sure and firm: The passages of Scripture in which God has revealed the dogmas have not been given obscurely or ambiguously; or, if there are any figures of speech in those passages, then they are immediately explained with an additional statement in Scripture itself, using clear and perspicuous words.

Therefore, let us acknowledge and consider with a grateful mind this benefit of the Son of God, that in those passages which present the doctrine concerning the essence and will of God, if there were any words, either figurative or otherwise obscure, which could have provided occasion for us somewhat unskilled and insufficiently trained men to fall into error, He Himself gave a clear and entirely unambiguous explanation with His own voice after the occasion and the question arose, as we see in Matthew 16, John 3, 4, and 6, and other passages.

Without a doubt, therefore, He would have done the same thing in the matter of the Supper, if He had wanted anything to be understood differently than the words sounded, especially since His disciples had not heard of that doctrine before, although it held so much importance for faith, as we have said. And if Christ had left behind in the Supper only figurative words, without any certain and clear statement, then His Apostles, at the very least, would have revealed both the figure of speech and its certain explanation after the Savior's ascension, just as in the other articles of faith they presented with clear and perspicuous words, without the shrouds of ambiguity, that doctrine which Christ had often cloaked behind the veil of figures. Nor should anyone imagine that the Apostles, who could have, with a single word, settled this inauspicious quarrel, intended to pass on a "bone of contention" (μῆλον ἔριδος), so that their hearers might not understand, although the sentence was added: "Whoever does not discern the body of the Lord eats judgment on himself." These things, carefully considered, furnish the most elegant and trustworthy arguments.

Fourth

Christ was instituting a mystery in the Supper which did not formerly exist in the Church, and was instituting it in such a way that

He wanted it to be understood, not only by those who were gifted with the extraordinary and peculiar gifts of the Holy Spirit (1 Cor. 12), but also by little children (Mat. 11)—indeed, by infants and nursing babes (Psa. 8), for He says, "which is shed, not only for you, but for many" (Mat. 26, Mark 14). For this reason, He undoubtedly spoke properly and clearly. For the interpretation of a figure of speech must always be founded on other proper and clear passages from which the interpretation of figurative language in the words of the Supper might be sought—such an interpretation, I say, in which the conscience may safely rest, since that particular mystery did not formerly exist in the Church. For the procedure of the original institution is one thing, and the procedure of the repeated inculcation is another. Indeed, it is certain that the dogmas as well as the commandments were often repeated with figurative words. But it is necessary that those words be explained elsewhere with proper and clear words, as Augustine says in Book 2, ch. 6, of *De Doctrina Christiana*. "Practically nothing is drawn from those obscurities which is not found to have been said most plainly elsewhere." And *Contra Epistulam Petiliani*, ch. 16: "The things which are said obscurely or ambiguously or figuratively cannot rightly be understood and explained unless those things which are said most plainly are held with a firm faith."

Fifth

It is beyond all controversy that Christ did something very significant at His last Supper. For He instituted a testamentary legacy, establishing how He wanted His beneficiaries to come into possession of His hereditary goods, which He was about to acquire by undergoing bitter death. Therefore, it is certain that, in this Supper, He did not intend to speak to His disciples in the same way as He spoke to the multitudes, through parables, so that the hearers should not understand (Mat. 13). Nor can the words of institution be related back to those passages of Scripture which, because of their obscurity, cultivate the zeal of the readers, and yet can be ignored without danger to faith. Nor was there a reason why He should couch in figurative language a practice that He wanted to continue in the Church until the end of the age. For, as Pirkeimerus rightly argues, no man, in establishing a testament, is so foolish as to take pains to obscure it or to speak in riddles. Rather, he painstakingly and with the greatest diligence sees to it that what he wants to be done after his death is free from all doubt and error. What impudence, then—or rather, what blasphemy—it is to assert that Christ, like a drunken man, in that mandate of His last will, which He painstakingly left behind and which He certainly wanted to be understood clearly (since He commanded that it be done in remembrance of Him until He comes), intended to speak so obscurely, without any clarification, that the minds of His heirs should be divided over His Testament into various understandings because of the ambiguous obscurity of the words! But the various and self-contradictory explanations of the Zwinglians clearly demonstrate that this only happens when the words are divorced from their proper meaning.

However, in no way did Christ say, "This do," in such a way that it is enough for us to do anything at all, whatever that may be. No, without any doubt, when He said, "Eat; this is My body. Drink; this is My blood," He intended only a single, definite meaning to be understood. But that single, definite, and necessary meaning cannot be established if a figure of speech is admitted, as is clear. For there always remains that notorious appendix, "It could also be explained in another way." Nor is it enough if everyone agrees on the negative proposition. But since it is an affirmative proposition, it must be asserted affirmatively with a single, certain, and necessary meaning what it is that is present and distributed in the Supper. Therefore, we take the words in a "literal sense," as they say, for we believe that Christ intended to be understood plainly, with a single, definite meaning.

Sixth

Figures of speech have this proper and peculiar trait, that anyone even moderately experienced in reading immediately recognizes them lying beneath the words. For example, "I am the Gate, the Vine; the Father is the Farmer, etc." Indeed, they are so obvious that even the crowds, when they heard Christ speaking in parables, although they did not perceive what He wanted to be understood, still recognized that something lay hidden under those figures of speech. But these words, "This is My body," first, do not provide in and of themselves any manifest or clear indication of a figure of speech. Second, the addition of the words, "which is given for you," excludes all suspicion of a figure of speech, unless the words are twisted in a truly forced manner. The truth is that the words "body and blood" are not found anywhere in the whole of Holy Scripture with the kind of meaning which is imagined by the Sacramentarians in the words of the Supper. And in such a great mystery, it is pure insolence to depart from the proper, clear, well-known, and customary meaning, supposing a novel and unusual interpretation based on one's own audacity, without the example of Scripture. This must not be tolerated.

Finally, I will add two elegant admonitions of the ancients. One is from Chrysostom's Homily 60: "Let us believe God at all times and let us not disagree with Him, even if what He says seems absurd to our sense and thinking and goes beyond both our sense and our reason. Let us do this in all things, and especially in the mysteries, not focusing only on those things which lie before our eyes, but also holding fast to His words. For we cannot be deceived by His words, while our sense can very easily be deceived. His words cannot be false, while our sense is deceived more and more often. Therefore, since He has said, 'This is My body,' let us not hold to it with any ambiguity, but let us believe and perceive it with the eyes of our intellect."

The other admonition is from Augustine, *De Doctrina Christiana,* Book 3, ch. 10, where he carefully admonishes that we should not immediately elude the clear character of the words with some figure of speech when the saying seems difficult to us. He says that this generally happens when Scripture affirms something which is inconsistent with the experience of the hearers, so that they immediately think that the saying must be figurative. Likewise, if the opinion of some error has preoccupied the mind and the Scripture asserts anything differently, the next way of escape, he says, is to say that it is a figure of speech, etc.

These arguments could easily be developed more broadly, and many others of this kind could be added. But consciences are more quickly overwhelmed than encouraged by a multitude of arguments, so I think that these things will suffice for the more simple-minded. This, then, is the analogy of sound interpretation which should be observed, as the Holy Spirit Himself has revealed in those passages wherein the dogmas are properly and principally founded. This analogy demonstrates the serious, sure, and firm reasons why one should not depart from the clear and certain character of the words in the matter of the Lord's Supper.

XII. Arguments from the collection and consensus of those Scripture passages in which the doctrine of the Lord's Supper is described and repeated.

These arguments which are taken from the perpetual analogy of sound interpretation are certainly able to encourage and strengthen consciences in their own right. But those arguments are more certain and illustrative which, in the collection and consensus of Scripture passages in which the doctrine of the Lord's

Supper is taught, are revealed so clearly and perspicuously that the simplest of men can recognize the certainty of a right faith from the true foundations. Yes, this is the only true and certain procedure in the dogmas of the faith. For when Peter says that the Scripture is not "of a private interpretation," he uses the very significant phrase ἰδίας ἐπιλύσεως. For thus the word is used in Mark 4. After Christ had spoken many things rather obscurely in parables, so that the crowds, although hearing, might not understand, He took the disciples aside and "interpreted" (ἐπέλυε) all things for them. And in Acts 19, "If there is a question about other things, it will be interpreted (ἐπιλυθήσεται) in a lawful assembly." Therefore, the sense of Peter's rule is this: If anything in Scripture seems obscure or controversial, each one should not devise the "interpretation" or ἐπίλυσιν of it from his own imaginations. But as Christ says in John 14, "The Holy Spirit, whom the Father will send in My name, He will teach you all things and remind you of all that I said to you."

Therefore, we should not expect peculiar enthusiasms and revelations by which that which is controversial may be settled and explained, as the fanatics of old—Montanus, Manes, and many others—falsely concluded. But the Holy Spirit has given His own true interpretation (ἐπίλυσιν) to the Church in the canonical Scriptures and has left it behind to be examined and sought in this way. For the same dogma, the same understanding and teaching is repeated in various passages of Scripture, sometimes with the same words, sometimes with different ones, so that faith may be strengthened and become more certain on the basis of the consistent testimony of many passages, and so that, if anything had previously been said either more briefly or more obscurely, it may be explained by a fuller and clearer statement of the Holy Spirit. This is what Jerome says in commenting on Isaiah 19: "It is the custom of the Scriptures to connect clear things with obscure things, and to set forth with a clear word what had previously been spoken enigmatically." Augustine discusses this rule in many passages of *De Doctrina Christiana*:

"Nothing in Scripture is so obscure that it is not explained more clearly in another place."

Therefore, since the doctrine of the Lord's Supper is not found in only one passage, but is repeated in several passages of Scripture, the Holy Spirit clearly did not want to subject it to anyone's private interpretation, but as in the rest of the dogmas, so also in this one He has reserved the interpretation (ἐπίλυσιν) for Himself and has revealed and passed it on to us by establishing a repetition of that same doctrine at various times in other passages of Scripture. Therefore, when something seems controversial in the doctrine of the Lord's Supper, or if anything has been said more briefly or more obscurely in one passage, it is certain that the true presentation of it is to be sought, not from one's private interpretation, but from other passages of Scripture where the same doctrine is found to be repeated for that very reason.

There is no better way to show how this should be done than with examples. Therefore, I will very briefly cite first one example, then another to make all this more plain.

Wycliffe and several others place that sentence, "John is Elijah," on the front line of battle in this discussion. *The bread is the body of Christ, just as John was Elijah.* But let us take a moment to examine that proposition according to Peter's rule. When the Son of God says in Matthew 11, "John is Elijah," should we immediately answer from the persuasive thoughts of our mind, "It isn't true! He can't be Elijah!"? Peter says for certain that the words of Scripture are not subject to private interpretation; instead, the certain and true interpretation (ἐπίλυσιν) of the Holy Spirit Himself must be sought.

But this is how the Spirit's interpretation is found. First, in Matthew 11, Christ does not simply say, "John is Elijah," but, "If you are willing to accept it." Second, He adds a clarifying statement, "He is Elijah who is to come." Therefore, this is not the Tishbite who lived during the reign of Ahab some 900 years (more or less) before the birth of John the Baptist, but the one whom Malachi prophesied would come, as Chrysostom wisely observed after weaving these circumstances together. Third, one should look around to see whether or not these sentences have been repeated in other passages of Scripture. In doing so, we find in John 1 that the negative is expressly stated: "I am not Elijah," says the Baptist. Fourth, in Luke 1, Gabriel makes the clearest statement of why the name Elijah is attributed to the Baptist, namely, not because of some sort of metempsychosis, but, "he will go before in the spirit and power of Elijah." With these clear statements, the Holy Spirit taught us His own interpretation (ἐπίλυσιν) of the proposition, "John is Elijah." And the conscience, strengthened by foundations of this kind, can safely depart from the words and rest in a figurative interpretation.

Therefore, since one must depart from the character of the words in that proposition, "John is Elijah," Scripture carefully and diligently teaches us the true interpretation, lest we speculate wildly about the sense. That being so, how much more diligently and clearly would this have to have been done in the propositions, "This is My body, this is My blood," if the Holy Spirit had wanted us to depart from the words and understand something else! For the proposition, "This is My body," is without any controversy more important than that saying, "John is Elijah." Nor is there equal danger in both cases if a false interpretation is admitted.

So also in Matthew 16, when Christ said, "Beware of the yeast of the Pharisees," He did not mean to furnish the Apostles with an obscure and ambiguous text, so to speak, leaving them to interpret the saying freely, according to their own thoughts. But since, on account of the figure of speech, the sense was somewhat more difficult and obscure, He permitted them to wonder and to dispute with one another concerning a "private interpretation" (ἐπίλυσιν), so that in this way He might have an occasion for revealing and teaching the true interpretation. Soon, therefore, He posits the negative: "I was not speaking to you about bread or about fermented dough." Furthermore, it should be considered whether that same phrase was repeated in another passage of Scripture. Indeed, we read it in Luke 12 with these words: "Watch out for the yeast of the Pharisees, which is hypocrisy." And from that interpretation, says Matthew, the Apostles understood that this saying was not about leavened bread, but about the doctrine of the Pharisees.

Also applicable here is the example of the promise made to Abraham, how God reiterated it on several occasions, explaining it ever more clearly and certainly when He saw that Abraham was speculating idly with his own private interpretation, as shown above.

I do not wish to add more examples at this time. I have only cited these so that one might use the examples to consider by what method and with what religious zeal and diligence one should seek the true and certain explanation of those words of the Lord's Supper which have now become so controversial, "This is My body, this is My blood." Therefore, since the dogma of the Lord's Supper is not only described in one passage of Scripture, but is repeated many times in several passages, it is clear that the true understanding and clarification of it must be sought on the basis of a comparison of said passages.

Now, if the Scripture had said, "It is not the body and blood of Christ," even as it said, "John is not Elijah, it is not leavened bread, it does not refer to an adopted offspring, etc.," then we would rightly and safely be able to abandon the character of the words and accept another interpretation. But if that interpretation (ἐπίλυσιν) of the Holy Spirit does not with certainty demonstrate and teach either the negative or any other interpretation, then it is clear what the conscience should believe and follow.

It really is a very simple matter if one merely pays attention to the chronology, which reveals a very lovely consensus, showing how those who wrote later on either confirmed the meaning by repetition or, with a certain explanation, passed on in writing those things which were first commanded concerning this dogma, so that they might thus have a simple and beautiful certainty of faith. It is certain, moreover, that Matthew, Mark, Luke, and Paul did not describe the institution of the Supper at one and the same time. And there is some variation among the history writers with regard to the number of years between them, for Irenaeus' commentary is rather obscure. Nicephorus says that the history of the Gospel began to be written down in the fifteenth year after Christ's ascension. But for the summary of the matter, there is no point in arguing over the minor points of the number of years, since, with regard to the order, it is agreed that Matthew wrote first, Mark second, Luke third, and Paul last. But I will follow the customary computation, which comes from Theophylact.

XIII. The description of the institution according to Matthew.

Matthew composed his history of the Gospel in the eighth year after the Savior's ascension and was the first to put the institution of the Lord's Supper in writing, as follows: "While they were eating, Jesus took bread; and when He had given thanks, He broke it and gave it to His disciples and said, 'Take, eat; this is My body.' And He took the cup, gave thanks and gave it to them, saying, 'Drink from it, all of you; this is My blood, which is of the New Testament, which is poured out for many for the remission of sins.'"

First we will consider the temporal circumstances in our description, for later on they will shed some light on the topic for us and provide us with a starting point for getting at the true and genuine sense of the institution.

Matthew says that Christ instituted the Lord's Supper while the disciples were eating, so it was certainly done during the Last Supper on the night in which Christ was betrayed. But whether it was done at the beginning of that Last Supper, or in the middle, or after it was finished, cannot be clearly determined from Matthew's description. Paul expressly says that it was done μετὰ τὸ δειπνῆσαι, that is, after that Last Supper was finished. And Luke, who was more careful than the rest to observe the order of things, as he promises in the introduction to his Gospel, divides up that Last Supper in this way: First, Christ ate the Passover with His disciples and undoubtedly observed the rite prescribed by God Himself in the Law (Exodus 12). He concluded that supper of the Old Testament with these words: "I say to you that from this time I will not eat it until it is fulfilled in the kingdom of God." Now, those who are experts in Hebrew cite from the ancient commentaries of the Jews, stating that the custom was observed as follows: They would eat the paschal lamb standing, with their loins girded and their staffs in their hands, etc. This was done quickly. Then, having loosened their belts and set down their staffs, they would sit down together for supper, in case anyone was still hungry or thirsty. This is the context in which Christ reclined, with John resting in His bosom, as Theophylact explains.

This order is clearly revealed in John 13, for it says that Christ got up from the supper, took off His garments and washed the disciples' feet—undoubtedly after they had removed their sandals—and reclined again and dipped the piece of bread. But according to the rite prescribed by God Himself, the paschal lamb was to be eaten quickly, with their loins girded, their sandals on their feet, and their staffs in their hands, etc., and we should not imagine that Christ violated that rite. Therefore, the things written in John 13 were done after the eating of the paschal lamb, and yet there was still a supper, for He reclined again, dipped the bread, etc. John thus proves the order of the Last Supper as we have described it, namely, that the sacred supper of the Old Testament was celebrated first, with the eating of the paschal lamb according to the Law. Afterward they sat down for the common supper, in case anyone was still hungry or thirsty. This is why it says that Christ washed His disciples' feet γενομένου δείπνου, after supper, that is, after the paschal supper was ended. He immediately adds that Jesus "rose from supper," that is, the supper which happened after the eating of the lamb. But Luke says that Christ also concluded that second supper, as well as the first, and that, indeed, He followed the common custom. For they write that it was customary for the Israelites in their solemn feasts that, when the supper was ended, the tables were then to be removed and the father of the family would take a cup, give thanks, distribute it to those who were gathered, and thus the feast was usually concluded. Luke clearly writes that Christ concluded the second supper in this same way. "And He took the cup, gave thanks, and said, 'Take and divide it among yourselves. For I say to you that I will not drink of the fruit of the vine until the kingdom of God comes.'" Finally, after the paschal lamb was eaten and that other subsequent supper was also concluded, Christ instituted that new and special supper which Paul calls the "Lord's Supper." And this is what Luke and Paul say, that it was "after supper," μετὰ τὸ δειπνῆσαι.

But why, you ask, have we so painstakingly emphasized this point? I reply: It is a beautiful observation, that the Son of God, in the very order of institution, separated by an obvious distinction His own Lord's Supper, which He was just then instituting, from all other feasts, whether common meals which fulfilled a natural necessity, or the feasts which were sacred types, as was the Old Testament eating of the paschal lamb, which served as a sign that taught about the past deliverance from Egypt and about the future redemption through Christ. And so the Zwinglian fabrication is destroyed when they say that the interpretation of these words, "This is My body," should be taken from the institution of the paschal lamb; likewise, when they claim that these words signify only that Christ is the food for the soul, even as bread nourishes the body. This meaning can also be observed in a certain common supper, as in John 6 the occasion for preaching about spiritual eating is taken from the five loaves of bread, and in John 4 a consideration of spiritual drinking is emphasized from the drinking of simple water. But Christ, in the very order of the institution, separated the Lord's Supper from all other foods, whether common or typical.

But let us finally address the description of the institution recorded in Matthew's Gospel. After the eating of the paschal lamb, and also after that other common supper was ended, "Jesus took bread, and, having given thanks, broke it and gave it to His disciples, saying, 'Take, eat.'" But what is this? He is not offering them common food, is He? Certainly not! For the common supper was concluded earlier. Surely it is not some kind of type, like the eating of unleavened bread? No, Christ had already earlier made an end to those "typical" foods. What is it, then, that He gives to the disciples? What is it that they take, if it is not common or typical food? Christ answers, "This which I give you, this which you take, is My body." These things are as clear as can be, unless we love the darkness more than the light of day. But since we have determined to seek the interpretation (ἐπίλυσιν) of the Holy Spirit on the basis of these words, let them be left well enough alone for the moment until we see the interpretation of the Holy Spirit Himself, understanding that, at this point, because of their brevity, certain things have not yet been sufficiently explained.

Indeed, in the description of the second part, Matthew uses very significant and clear words, and an inspection of them will prove most delightful. For Matthew alone uses the causal conjunction, the redditive τοῦτο γάρ, "*For* this is My blood." This agrees beautifully with the description given above about the order of the Last Supper. For after the supper was ended, both the paschal and the common, Christ gave the disciples the cup. He commanded them all to drink from that one cup, and the particle γάρ explains the reason: "Drink," not to quench your thirst, for that drinking had already been concluded, nor that it might serve as some kind of sign pointing to something else, for Christ had already concluded the typical supper earlier, saying that He would not drink of it again from then on. What is it, then, that they are commanded to drink, now that the supper is concluded? Christ gives the reason for it with the particle γάρ: "Drink, *for* this is My blood." Matthew here does not write with that more obscure brevity which he had used in the description of the first part, saying, "This is My body." He adds a statement about what kind of blood it is which is being distributed and received in that cup. "For this is My blood, which is of the New Testament, which is shed for many for the remission of sins."

A consideration of the circumstances adds to the beauty of it. A little earlier, in the eating of the paschal lamb, they had the blood of the Old Testament. With this, He now contrasts His own blood, which is of the New Testament. Now it is most certain that the blood of the New Testament is not the blood of bulls and goats, Heb. 9 and 10, much less is it the fruit of the vine. No, it is the very blood of Christ, Heb. 9 and 13, 1 Pet. 1, Zec. 9, etc. Now, if you ask, not for the sake or arguing, but for the sake of learning, what it is that is present, given, and received in that cup, Christ answers, "It is My blood." And so that no doubt may remain as to what kind of blood it is, the statement is added, "It is My blood, which is of the New Testament." In Hebrews 9, the Scripture says that the blood of the New Testament is not someone else's blood, but is the very blood of Jesus Christ, the eternal High Priest. If, then, we seek the truth with godly zeal, asking what it is that is given and received in that cup, what else could we be looking for when we have a declaration as clear as this?

But each one of the words is understood more clearly from the antithesis. The blood of the paschal lamb is the blood of the Old Testament, but "this is My blood, which is of the New Testament." In eating the paschal lamb, it was done by the shedding of blood, as the Epistle to the Hebrews says in chapter 11, "for that family which slaughtered it for their bodily deliverance" (Exodus 12). But "this blood of Mine, which I am giving to you, which you are receiving, will be shed for many, and that, for the remission of sins." The blood of the Old Testament also was not one and the same, but sometimes it was the blood of a lamb (Exodus 12), sometimes of calves (Exodus 24), sometimes of bulls and goats (Heb. 10). But the blood of the New Testament is only and solely that which Jesus Christ sheds for the remission of sins. Therefore, no one should make up his own special interpretation of the words, "This is My blood." Likewise, the application of the blood of the Old Testament was done either by sprinkling (Exo. 24 and Heb. 9), or by smearing it on the doorframes of their houses (Exo. 12). In fact, the application of the blood which is of the New Testament actually happens by faith alone, apart from the use of the Supper (1 Pet. 1). But in the Supper, Christ instituted a clearly new and special manner of application: "Drink, for this is My blood." And in order to show clearly that there should be a distinction between the application of the blood of the Old and New Testaments, He says, "Drink." For in the Old Testament, it was forbidden to use blood, both in food and in drink, as Augustine also noted. This antithesis very nicely and very clearly demonstrates that the saying, "This is My blood," is not like the saying in Genesis 49, "He will wash his cloak in the blood of the grape." Or in Isaiah 1, "Your hands are full of blood." Or in Psalm 51, "Deliver me from bloods.[2]" For a statement is added explaining what kind of blood is being given to those who drink in the cup of the Lord's Supper. And that fuller declaration about the blood is correctly directed backwards to clarify the brevity that was used in the first part ("This is My body"). For if the blood of Christ is truly and substantially present and distributed in the cup, then the same reason will apply to the bread when it is said, "This is My body," according to that antithesis. "Earlier you ate the flesh of the lamb. But now what I am giving you to eat, this is My body."

2 cf. Vulgate

And since these things are so clear, they should really satisfy those who are piously seeking the truth, even if no other declaration had been handed down in Scripture. But since, after Matthew's history was written down, the Holy Spirit instituted the repetition of that same doctrine at later times, in other passages of Scripture, let us attend to that order that we may have a more certain and fuller confirmation of our faith.

XIV. Mark's description.

Mark wrote his Gospel account in the second year after Matthew wrote his; namely, in the tenth year after Christ's ascension. And it is evident that, in that repetition, the Holy Spirit declared many things more fully and more clearly which were said more obscurely in Matthew's Gospel. For example, Matthew had said, "The blasphemy against the Spirit will not be forgiven, neither in this age nor in the one to come." Mark puts it this way: "He will never have forgiveness, but will be guilty of eternal judgment." So, too, Matthew had said, "With difficulty will the rich enter the kingdom of heaven." Lest this should be understood concerning the superstitious abandonment of one's resources, Mark adds a clear declaration in his repetition of that account, wherein Jesus says to His disciples, "'How hard it will be for those who have riches to enter God's kingdom!' And the disciples were astonished at His words. But Jesus again responded, saying, 'Little children, how hard it is for those who trust in riches to enter into God's kingdom!'" Therefore, since the Holy Spirit also instituted a repetition of the doctrine of the Lord's Supper in Mark's Gospel, this was certainly not a useless tautology; Scripture wanted both to confirm and to clarify the things previously stated by means of the subsequent repetitions.

So let us consider the repetition of the institution in Mark. Indeed, it is clear that in Mark's repetition, he wanted to bring in some clarification. For instead of saying, "He gave thanks," he has, "He blessed," which is also the word Paul borrowed from Mark in 1 Corinthians 10. He also says that the disciples did what they were commanded: they all drank from it. But in those words concerning which the controversy now exists, he changes nothing. He neither substitutes the negative, "It is not My blood," as we said about that other statement, "I am not Elijah"; nor does he add anything that either reveals or clarifies a figure of speech. No, he retains the same words, down to the syllable, "This is My body. This is My blood, which is of the New Testament, etc."

But the Zwinglians insist that nothing can be proven from this repetition. For since those words which are controversial are repeated in those two places with the same syllables, the matter is equally obscure, as if they were only found in a single passage. But as for us, let us listen to Paul, the most certain witness as to what conclusion we should reach from repetitions of this kind which occur in the Scriptures with the same words. This is what he says in Philippians 3: "It certainly is not tedious for me to write the same things to you, but it renders you certain." He uses the word ἀσφαλές, which signifies such a certainty in the true understanding that we are not borne about by any wind of doctrine, through the cunning of men, but that we are able to rest safely in the demonstrated and repeated understanding. For thus it is used in Luke 1, Acts 21, and Acts 25. Therefore, we have Paul for the most substantial witness of the fact that when in Scripture the same dogma is repeated with the same words, it is done so that, by that repetition of the same words, the certainty of our faith may be confirmed in such a way that we can rest safely on the simple and proper understanding in the face of any winds of argumentation. For if the Holy Spirit wanted us to understand something different than what the words say, He would also present it with different words. He would not use the exact same words in the repetition. Therefore, Mark, by the very fact that he merely repeats the same words which are found in Matthew, furnishes a notable and sufficiently firm argument that we are not to depart from the character of the words.

But since the matter is lofty and the disputation arduous, of which it is said, "Whoever does not discern the Lord's body eats judgment on himself," the Holy Spirit has given a still fuller and more certain explanation. And we should embrace that enormous benefit of the Son of God with a grateful mind and consider that in the very words of institution, He, with paternal concern for His Church, wanted to see to it that there would be no need to fluctuate between uncertain interpretations with ambiguous conjectures, but that, if we are willing to follow the voice of the Holy Spirit as He dictates, we would be able to have a certain, more certain, and most certain interpretation of what it is that is present, given, and received in the Supper.

XV. The repetition of the institution according to Luke.

Luke is third, after Matthew and Mark. He instituted his repetition of the institution of the Lord's Supper in the fifteenth year after Christ's ascension. At the beginning of his Gospel, he promises that in his writing he will more carefully describe things than had previously been done by others, and Paul proves this with his own testimony when he says of Luke, "whose praise is in the Gospel throughout all the churches." Clearly it was for this very reason that, after the descriptions given by Matthew and Mark, the Holy Spirit instituted in Luke's Gospel a repetition of the institution of the Lord's Supper so that those things which had been said by the others either more briefly or more obscurely might be explained with a certain and, in a sense, fuller elaboration. For Luke recounts more succinctly those things which had previously been described by the other Evangelists quite brilliantly. For example, in the description of the second part, those phrases—"having given thanks, He gave them, etc., drink from it, all of you, etc., for the remission of sins, etc."—are not added in Luke's account. For he wanted his words to be read in such a way that they would be compared with the descriptions of the other Gospels, which were already extant in the Church at that time. But he adds certain things which are not there in the descriptions of the institution according to Matthew and Mark, and this was certainly done to clarify the obscurity which the brevity of the other writers could have produced among their posterity, so that all ambiguity might be removed and that the path toward future corruptions might be blocked. For since it could not be clearly understood from the descriptions of Matthew and Mark whether that command about the Lord's Supper was merely personal, as when Peter was commanded to walk on water, or whether it was universal, pertaining to the whole Church in the New Testament, Luke adds these words in the description of the first part: "This do in remembrance of Me." And in the description of the second part, he expressly mentions the temporal circumstance, namely, "after supper." Likewise, Luke links the demonstrative pronoun τοῦτο, which could have been twisted to refer to something else in Matthew and Mark, to a definite antecedent, for he says that it pertains to that which was being offered and received, saying, τοῦτο τὸ ποτήριον, "*This cup* is the New Testament in My blood, which is shed for you."

Therefore, let us do what godly men once did in Asia Minor. When Cerinthus tried with venom to usurp the title of tradition for his blasphemy and craftily twisted the writings of the other Evangelists to support his own opinion, those godly men and lovers of the truth went to the Apostle John, asking him to clarify the accounts of the others with his own confession. Since these words ("This is My body. This is My blood.") are now being brought into controversy, let us go to consult Luke, so that he who has clarified the understanding of the institution of the Supper in many other passages may also teach us the true interpretation of the Holy Spirit Himself concerning these words.

Let us learn, moreover, to recognize the exegetical phrase which is used in Scripture when it adds something for the sake of clarification. For example, the rest of the Evangelists call Christ "God" and "the Son of God." But since those words were being distorted due to their ambiguity, as Moses is the "god" of Aaron, and as the magistrates are called "gods," John delivers a certain clarification through just such an addition: He is the God "through whom all things were made." Likewise, He is "the only-begotten Son who is in the Father's bosom." Indeed, it is clear how much weight these additions have in that highly important article. In the same way, that statement, "John is Elijah," would be both obscure and ambiguous. But through the addition of the phrase, "who is to come," it is clarified in such a way that the sense is plain, free of ambiguity. And in Luke 12, "Beware of the leaven of the Pharisees ἥτις ἐστὶν ὑπόκρισις, which is hypocrisy." In this passage, there is no one who fails to see that, to words which were rather obscure on their own, a certain clarification was added in that little phrase attached at the end.

Therefore, in his description of the words of the Supper, Luke uses that very exegetical phrase to show us and teach us the true and certain explanation of the Holy Spirit Himself concerning those words, "This is My body." For he writes, "This is My body, which is given for you." Now, the phrase, "the body of Christ," is used with three meanings in Scripture. First, it signifies the substance of Christ's flesh, which was conceived by the Holy Spirit and born of the Virgin Mary. Second, it signifies the mystical body of Christ; that is, the Church. Third, it is also used in Colossians 2 in this way, "...which are a shadow of the things to come, but the body of Christ." Now, when Paul says in Colossians 1, "the body of Christ," and adds, "which is the Church," no one argues or disputes any longer about the proper understanding. So when Matthew and Mark say, "This is My body," and Luke adds, "which is given for you," the statement is absolutely clear, unless we wanted to be blind, with our eyes closed under the most brilliant light. For it is not a sign of an absent body that was given for us, nor the efficacy of an absent body, but (as Paul says in Colossians 1) "the body of Christ's flesh"; that is, that very substance which was conceived by the Holy Spirit, born of the Virgin Mary, etc. Now, if you ask, with the intention of learning, what is present, given, and received with the bread in the Lord's Supper, Luke responds with words that are not at all obscure or ambiguous, "It is that body of Christ which was given for us." Therefore, it is present not only symbolically or merely effectively, but truly and substantially.

Similarly, in the description of the cup, Luke transposes the word order for the sake of certainly and clarity. For where Matthew and Mark say, "This is My blood, which is of the New Testament," Luke says, "This cup is the New Testament in My blood." Now, with these words of Luke it must be that one and the very same meaning is being expressed as is contained in the words of Matthew and Mark. But why did he transpose the word order in this way? I reply: Luke knew very well that the descriptions of the others were already present in the Church, and he wanted his description to be compared with theirs so that no other interpretation should be accepted but that which comes from the school of the Holy Spirit Himself, through a comparison of Scripture passages. And in that transposition, the Holy Spirit zealously wished to guide the words in such a way that no craftiness would permit the words to be explained any differently than in their proper meaning. For if anyone wanted to take the blood figuratively in Matthew and Mark, Luke and Paul by no means allow it. Nor can the New Testament in Luke's and Paul's accounts be separated from its proper meaning through any figure of speech, for Matthew and Mark oppose such an understanding, as Luther magnificently deduced.

Therefore, Luke says that with that cup the New Testament is being given to those who drink and is being received by them—the New Testament which is described in this way in Jeremiah 31: "I will be propitious toward their iniquity, and their sin I will remember no longer. I will be their God, and they will be My people." But how is the cup the New Testament? Could it be because we drink wine from it? Certainly not! But it is "in My blood," as Matthew and Mark say. "For that which you receive and drink is My blood which is of the New Testament." Thus, by a magnificent consensus, the Evangelists clarify and shed light on one another.

Up to this point, we have spoken about the consensus of the three Evangelists. It cannot fail to delight and to greatly confirm the mind that piously seeks the simple truth, how the Holy Spirit, with careful diligence, has shown such genuine consideration for His Church in the words of the Supper, how He always either confirms or clarifies in later repetitions the things previously said, so that we might be able to be certain about the sense from that clarification of the Holy Spirit which He has manifestly demonstrated and passed on in the repetition of the institution. Why, then, have we, by arguing and questioning, insolently covered up those things which the Holy Spirit so obviously wanted to be most plainly explained with His very own voice? Indeed, the clarifications of which we have spoken until now are so clear that they should have satisfied everyone, so that we should not seek, discuss, or desire anything further. But in order that the genuine faith in this great mystery may be fully explained and firmly grounded, the witness of Paul has also been added.

XVI. The words and sentences of Paul.

The institution of the Supper was repeated a fourth time, after the Evangelists, by the Apostle Paul in 1 Corinthians, around A.D. 54. The authority of the Pauline testimony in this controversy is very great, for many reasons.

First, as Augustine says, *De opera Monachorum*, chapter 7: "The Lord indeed spoke in parables and analogies, as the Evangelists described. But the Apostle, in true apostolic form, discusses things more openly and speaks more properly than figuratively, as many things—indeed, practically all things—are found in the apostolic epistles, etc." In fact, this is the command Christ gave the Apostles in Matthew 10, "What I say to you in the dark, speak in the light."

Second, Paul says that he is the teacher of the Gentiles. Now, the Apostles and most of the rest of the converts from the Jews would have been able to see and understand on their own a figure of speech in the words of the Supper without anyone to point it out to them, since they were accustomed to the figures in the Law. But surely the plain, proper, and perspicuous explanation would have had to have been passed on to the Gentiles, who were not accustomed to those figures, if anything were to be understood differently than the words sound. Therefore, Paul would surely have done that in his repetition, since he professes to be the teacher of the Gentiles.

Third, he says that he is a debtor, not only to the wise, but also to the unwise. Therefore, Paul was compelled also to take them into account, lest the less educated among them, due to their slowness, should idly speculate about the figurative language if he used it without a manifest clarification, just as now the figurative interpreters of the words of the Supper cannot even agree among themselves.

Fourth, Paul is not merely giving a historical recitation of the words of institution, as the Evangelists do, but since the Corinthians themselves had indicated to him that certain abuses and controversies had already begun to arise concerning this Sacrament, he sets forth his recitation of the institution as a steadfast rule according to which all such controversies both should and rightly could be decided. Indeed, how foolish it would have been for him to set down that rule, and especially for such an intended use, with obscure and ambiguous words, so that those who had asked him for his counsel were even more uncertain afterwards than they were before, as he himself says. Indeed, since the doctrine of the Lord's Supper had already, within such a short time, begun to be distorted in that church whose foundations Paul himself had laid only a year and a half earlier, he undoubtedly foresaw in the Spirit that much more grievous conflicts would arise concerning this mystery in later times. For that reason, he did not only institute a repetition of the institution for the sake of the Corinthians, but he wanted to demonstrate and deliver to the generations to come the steadfast norm and rule of the genuine faith and of the steadfast adjudication of all questions and controversies concerning the Lord's Supper.

Fifth, it is absolutely clear that Paul, in his repetition of the institution, clarified those things which were more obscure in the descriptions of the others. For example, when Luke said, "This do, etc.," it could have been seen as being said only to the Apostles. But Paul says that it pertains to the whole Church, all the way up to Judgment Day, "until He comes." Likewise, it could not be clearly understood from Luke whether it was to be done only once, as in Baptism. But Paul says, "As often as, etc." And he expressly explains what the remembrance is: "You will proclaim the Lord's death, etc." Undoubtedly, then, he would have handed down a similar clarification concerning the words, "This is My body, etc.," if he had meant anything to be understood differently than the words sound, since he was such a careful interpreter in the other things, and since it is certain that, in those words, "This is My body, etc.," the chief thing in the Lord's Supper is contained, and since Paul himself says, "Whoever does not discern the Lord's body eats judgment." Nor would the plain words have been lacking to him by which he could have described the presence of the vigor or efficacy of the body and blood of Christ, without the presence of the substance, if he had wanted it to be understood that way. For he often speaks in this way elsewhere, as in 1 Corinthians 5: "Being absent in body, but present in spirit, I have already decided as if present, etc." And in Colossians 2: "Although I am absent in the flesh, yet I am with you in spirit." If Paul had spoken in this way about the body of Christ in the Supper, it would have been clear that it was a metaphor. But now in the description of the second part, he repeats the same words which Luke had used, "This cup is the New Testament in My blood." But why does he not add those words, "which is shed for you for the remission of sins"? These words are not useless, are they? Surely no sane person would say so! But this is a magnificent observation. When Paul wants to add some clarification to the descriptions of the Evangelists, he then adds certain words, such as, "As often as, etc." "Proclaim the Lord's death, etc." "Until He comes, etc." Therefore, when he speaks with more brevity and omits some words, he indicates that those things have been described clearly and properly by the Evangelists and should be sought from them. With this in mind, he omits those verbs in the second part, "When He had given thanks, He gave them, etc." Drink from it, all of you, etc." "Which is shed for you for the remission of sins, etc." Thus we have an argument that those words are not to be understood differently than they sound, as in a well-known, clear, and proper understanding. For Paul himself says in Phi. 3 that when the same things are repeated, it is a confirmation of the certainty of them. But in the first part, he does not merely repeat the same words, but for the sake of clarification, he writes "is broken" instead of "is given" in order to show with certainty that the body which is present, given, and received in the Supper is none other than the body which was given for us on the altar of the cross. Yes, the same body which was given for us is also distributed for us in the Supper. For this is what "to break" means, according to the customary usage of Scripture. This comparison of the words of Luke and Paul is truly magnificent! Luke says, "the body which is given for you." Surely it was the true and substantial body of Christ that was given for us! Now Paul says that the same body "is broken," that is, "is distributed" in the Lord's Supper. "This is My body, which is broken for you." If anyone is not moved by this clear and immovable truth, he must truly be blind (2 Cor. 4)! As for me, this magnificent consensus in the repetition of the institution delights, encourages, and confirms me, and with all my heart I give thanks to the Son of God, our Lord Jesus Christ, for those sweet clarifications which He has given us through His Holy Spirit at various times in the repetitions of the institution. And I pray that He would preserve me in that simple and well-established faith against all corruptions. Amen.

Up to now, from the repetition of the institution which was made at four different times in four different places, we have shown the magnificent and steadfast arguments demonstrating that one should not depart from the grammatical character of the words, "This is My body. This is My blood."

There are still three passages in which the doctrine of the Lord's Supper is repeated in such a way that both arguments and exhortations are drawn from them, and therefore these passages are able to reveal the true and native understanding, because it is necessary that those passages from which the exhortations and arguments are drawn must be certain and clear in their sense. The passages are these: 1 Corinthians 11, "He will be guilty of the body and blood of the Lord." Likewise, "Not discerning the Lord's body." 1 Corinthians 10, "The bread which we break, etc." For if these passages also provide a clear testimony that the character of the words must be retained, then we will truly be able to boast with Paul, "We have the mind of Christ" (1 Cor. 2). As we demonstrated above, this is the status of the entire dispute.

Indeed, those two statements from 1 Corinthians 11—"He will be guilty of the body and blood of the Lord," and "Not discerning the Lord's body, etc."—so strongly and clearly prove that we are not to depart from the native character of the words that even Oecolampadius rejects those who seek figures of speech there, explaining the word "body" as a symbol of the body. For he says, "The word 'body' is taken in its proper meaning in these verses, 'He will be guilty of the body and blood of the Lord.' And, 'Not discerning the Lord's body.'" But it is utterly certain that Paul, in these passages, is speaking of no other body than the one of which it is said in the institution, "This is My body." If, then, it is asked what is present, given, and received in the Supper, Christ responds, "This is My body." And Paul also demonstrates in these verses, by the admission of the adversaries themselves, that the word "body" is to be understood properly. This is the very point we were compelled to prove.

The arguments will be even clearer if the grammar is considered more closely. To his fully developed description of the institution, Paul attaches this statement by way of inference: "Therefore, whoever eats this bread and drinks the cup of the Lord in an unworthy manner will be guilty of the body and blood of the Lord." But why? For what reason? This is shown by the illative particle. For Christ, the Son of God, says of that which is eaten and drunk in an unworthy manner, "This is My body. This is My blood." For the word ἔνοχος, "guilty," in its own construction either expresses the kind of punishment or describes the reason for which liability to punishment has been contracted. We will not argue here about that distinction grammarians make, saying that the genitive indicates guilt while the dative indicates punishment, for this difference is never observed in the writings of the Apostles. But, in any case, there is no need to argue over this, for when Paul says, "He will be guilty of the body and blood of the Lord," it is clear that it is not the kind of punishment that is being described, but the fact of, and the reason for, the liability to that punishment which is expressed later; namely, the judgment of damnation. Therefore, he does not say that the man who eats unworthily is guilty of the bread, but of the body of the Lord. In other words, not the bread, but the body of the Lord which was given for us is that thing by whose unworthy eating guilt is contracted for judgment, for that which is distributed and received is the body of the Lord. Therefore, it is certain that those of whom Paul is speaking become guilty of the body and blood of the Lord from the unworthy eating of that thing which is present, distributed, and received in the Lord's Supper. If you ask, "What is that thing?," Paul answers that it is "the body of the Lord," and that it is received in the Supper, not only by those who, in sincere repentance, apply the merits of Christ to themselves by a true faith, but also by those who eat unworthily. For the distribution and the reception are combined, since He gave it to them saying, "Take, eat." These things are obvious.

The second statement is, "He eats judgment on himself, not discerning (διακρίνων) the body of the Lord." The term διακρίνω means to consider the quality or worthiness of something and then to remove or separate it from the other things, from the common class, as it were, in such a way that it is considered and treated more honorably than the other things. Thus, when the Epistle of Jude commands that sinners should not all be treated in the same way, but that the curable should be treated one way, the intractable another, it uses this word διακρινόμενοι. And in Acts 15 Peter says, "Since God gave the Holy Spirit to the Gentiles as well as to us, therefore He has made no distinction between us and them." Now, Paul, with his statement, is not speaking about those who think in an ungodly way about the humanity of Christ, but about that discernment which is made in the eating of the bread of the Lord's Supper, of which Christ says, "This is My body." Therefore, that thing which is present, distributed, received, and eaten in the Supper must be discerned. But Paul does not say that the bread must be discerned, since it has been added to the mysteries, like the showbread; he says, "the Lord's body." Therefore, let a man examine himself by means of this discernment, so that he considers what and how great that thing is which is present, distributed, and received with the bread in the Supper. And since Christ says that it is His body, Paul draws a serious warning from that fact. Therefore, whoever in the act of eating does not discern that body which is present, distributed, and received, but treats it with no greater reverence than if he were receiving merely the bread that has come from the baker, or perhaps some of the showbread, he eats unworthily, for judgment. The text manifestly reveals this understanding and agrees beautifully with the things that have been said up until now. So, too, Ambrose says,

"Let a person approach the Communion with fear, so that the mind knows that it owes reverence to Him whose body he approaches to receive. For he should discern within himself that it is the Lord whose blood he drinks in this mystery."

The third passage is found in 1 Corinthians 10: "The bread which we break, is it not the communion of the body of Christ?" Luther says that this passage was for him a living antidote in these controversies, for it was also mutilated in several ways by the Zwinglians. Zwingli says that this communion is merely an external symbol that those who are receiving it are members in the fellowship of the body of the Church. But then it would logically follow that the body of the Church was given for us. Oecolampadius says that it is only a symbol that we have all been redeemed at the price of one body. But how do these things agree with the text? Now, they cleverly and insidiously play games with the word "communion," claiming that, when Paul recited the words of institution, he did not want to change anything with regard to the rite; but he gave the interpretation in 1 Corinthians 10, namely, that the body is not to be understood about the substance of Christ's flesh, but about the communion of the body, that is, that the recipients are receiving the right to become partakers of all the merits of the body of Christ. But they claim that the substance itself of Christ's body is not present or distributed in the Supper, but only the communion of an absent body. We will address the words later; first we will address the matter itself. For if they want to thrust that interpretation on us, they will first have to prove by clear testimonies of Scripture that with the word "communion" Paul is removing and excluding the actual substance of the body of Christ from the Supper, and that a communion separate from the substance of Christ's body is present and offered in the Supper.

Now, there are three firm arguments against this exposition. First, the spiritual communion is only of those who truly believe, and it always takes place for eternal life. But in the Lord's Supper, the bread which we break is the communion of the body of *Christ*, not only with those who eat worthily for eternal salvation, but also with those who eat unworthily for judgment and eternal damnation, for they eat and drink judgment on themselves. Therefore, the Zwinglian interpretation does not stand. Otherwise, no one could eat judgment on himself. Second, if you wish to be certain whether or not the substance of Christ's body is excluded from the Supper by the word "communion," consider that Paul says, "I speak as to wise men. Judge for yourselves what I say. The bread which we break, etc." But on what basis are they to judge this sentence? Surely from the doctrine of the Lord's Supper which he had previously passed on to them. "I received from the Lord what I also passed on to you, etc." Therefore, the "communion" of the body of Christ and, "This is My body," must be the same thing which is broken for you. Indeed, the first sentence is to be judged from the words of institution, for two things are done in the Supper. There is a breaking and a communion; that is, something is distributed and received. Indeed, we see the bread which is distributed. But the question is, is it only bread which is distributed and received? Paul says, "It is not only bread that is being given to those who eat, but the bread is the participation of the body of Christ, just as it is described in the institution. That which you receive is My body which is distributed for you." Third, Paul ascribes to the bread the communion of the body of Christ, and to the cup the communion of His blood. But Scripture does not divide the merits of Christ in such a way that some things are attributed to His body, others to His blood. Therefore, as the institution shows, the communion is to be understood concerning the substance of the body and blood of Christ. Nor does the word "communion" have the force or emphasis of removing the presence of the substance. For in 2 Corinthians 13, Paul uses the same word. "The communion of the Holy Spirit be with you." Shall we say, then, that Paul agrees with those who imagined that the Holy Spirit dwells in believers, not according to His essence, but only with His gifts and virtue, like saying, "The sun is in the field"?

These things are clear and sure, but they play tricks with the word "communion." *Es sey ein Gemeinschafft mit oder an dem leib Christi.* "It is a fellowship with or in the body of Christ." But the grammar shows that this is a manifest corruption, for there is a difference between these statements—Philippians 1, κοινωνία εἰς τὸ εὐαγγέλιον, "communion in the Gospel"; 1 John 1, κοινωνία μετὰ τοῦ πατρὸς καὶ υἱοῦ, "communion with the Father and the Son"—and the statement here, κοινωνία, "communion of the body and blood of Christ." It does not say, "with" the body, or "in" the blood.

It is very customary in Scripture to use the word κοινωνία for that which is distributed and communicated to the poor (Romans 15, 2 Corinthians 8 & 9, Hebrews 13, etc.). And Paul himself soon explains the word κοινωνία when he says, "We all partake (μετέχομεν) of the one bread," not because we merely have a right in that bread, but because all of us in common receive from it. Thus it is more correctly and more significantly rendered a "partaking," by which the body of Christ is communicated, as Hilary nicely refers to it as "the Sacrament of the communicated flesh and blood." For thus it agrees with the words of institution, "This is My body which is broken, that is, distributed for you." Luther himself complains that the word *Gemeinschafft*, "fellowship," is not proper in this passage, but that he was unable to find anything better. Therefore, Paul does not use the word κοινωνία to remove the substance of the body and blood of the Lord from the Supper, just as he does not deny that the Holy Spirit dwells in the bodies of believers when he says in 2 Corinthians 13, "The κοινωνία of the Holy Spirit be with you." So then, there is a notable and lovely consensus of this statement of Paul with the proper and native understanding of the words of institution.

These are the passages of Scripture in which the doctrine of the Lord's Supper is both described and repeated. We have shown, moreover, from the manifest consensus of those passages that we have no sufficiently certain and firm reasons to depart from the proper and native meaning of these words, "This is My body. This is My blood." This is the status of the dispute, as noted above, which, having been correctly set forth, clarifies many things, as noted below.

It is certain that something is present and offered in the Lord's Supper. Christ commands us to receive something. And when He says, "Eat, drink," He shows how we should receive it. If someone asks what it is, Christ answers, "This is My body. This is My blood." If these words are to be taken in their proper and native sense, the matter is plain and clear. That is what we have demonstrated thus far.

It is worthy of consideration that Christ guided those words in such a way that they cannot be eluded by a figure of speech. For first, since **Carlstadt** cut the pronoun "this" away from the antecedent, that is, from the bread which is offered, Luke immediately refuted this invention, saying, "This cup, etc." Second, **Zwingli** found a figure of speech in the verb "is." But Luke omitted the word "is" in the second part. "This cup the New Testament in My blood, etc." The verb "is" is also missing from the phrase, "not discerning the body of the Lord, etc." Third, **Oecolampadius** interprets the body as the symbol of the body. But Luke says that it is that body which was given for us. Surely it was not a ghost that was crucified for us! Fourth, **Peter Martyr** [Vermigli] inverts the word order: "My body is this"; namely, this food. But Luke does not allow this. "The New Testament in My blood is this cup," made, perhaps, of clay of or wood. Fifth, **Calvin** explains the body as the efficacy and vigor of the absent body for salvation. But Paul says that those who eat unworthily eat judgment on themselves. And surely the efficacy of the absent body was not given for us. Thus, the words have been fortified on all sides by their own character.

Once the true sense has been established and proven, Paul's rules in 1 Timothy 6, as we mentioned above, should always be added; namely, that we should not allow ourselves to be diverted from the simple and true sense just because we are unable to disentangle every detail, neither through objections nor through questions. Nor should one seek to accumulate many irrelevant testimonies and arguments, but let the simplicity which has certain and clear foundations suffice. For Pirkeimerus correctly writes against Oecolampadius, "Your arguments are too meticulous and passionate as you wrestle anxiously over every single detail, rendering your cause suspect to all men." Likewise, "That splendid and artificial pomp is the truest sign of your spirit; it undoubtedly proceeds from a burdened and anxious conscience. For Quintilian also says, 'The use of many arguments dispels faith in the preparations themselves,' etc."

XVII. The testimonies of the ancients.

Now that sure and firm foundations have been laid from the Holy Spirit's own clarification, of whom it is written, "No one knows the things that are of God except the Spirit of God," it is not unhelpful to consider also the testimonies of the ancient and purer Church. For even though faith does not depend on human authority, we do believe in the Catholic Church in which the Son of God at all times gives certain scribes, trained for the kingdom of heaven. He wants their unanimous confession to be consumed and proclaimed, and He wants it to stand, so that succeeding generations may be encouraged and strengthened. Therefore, after godly minds have been built upon the foundation of the Prophets and Apostles, they are strengthened even more by the confession of those who judge rightly. Moreover, the determinations of the ancients concerning this controversy have been collected by the most excellent men of singular judgment, so that a person labors in vain if he tries to amass many other statements. For testimonies are not to be numbered, but pondered. But since the adversaries only do this in order to accumulate many dissimilar statements from the writings of the Fathers and to elude the clearest of testimonies with their clever interpretation, I will only note some general observations from the statements of the Fathers from which it can clearly and definitively be concluded against all corruptions that they spoke about the bodily presence, not about the sign alone or the efficacy of the absent body and blood in the Supper. As Augustine says in Bk. 1, *Contra Iulianum*: "Before the controversies of the Pelagians arose, the Fathers spoke less warily about original sin." There is no doubt that this also happened occasionally in the matter of the Eucharist, since in this area the ancients had no adversaries to deal with, so that it is not difficult to find ambiguous, obscure, and dissimilar statements in their writings by which consciences are more disturbed than edified. For sometimes they speak of external signs in the Supper. They speak often about a spiritual communion. At times, they speak about that which is present and distributed with the external signs in the Supper. If those statements are mingled together, it easily creates confusion. Therefore, it is useful to have such observations at the ready which both show with certainty the genuine understanding of the ancients and which can correctly be set against the many dissimilar and less helpful sayings when they are amassed.

First. The whole of antiquity affirms with great consensus that Christ is in us and dwells in us, that He is joined and united with us, not only spiritually, by faith and love through the Holy Spirit, but also bodily, naturally, by natural participation, by bodily union, and they say that this is done in the use of the Lord's Supper. Passages are found in Cyril: *In Ioan.*, Bk. 10, ch. 13; Bk. 11, chs. 26 & 27; Bk. 4, ch. 16. In Chrysostom: Homily 83 on Matthew, Homily 45 on John, Homily 60 & 61 *Ad Populum Antiocheum*. In Hilary: Bk. 8 *De Trinitate*. Now, the ancients do not mean to say that there is no need for faith or the Holy Spirit in the salutary use of the Supper. For Cyril clearly says that faith is required, commenting on John 6. But they are looking at the passage in Ephesians 3 where the spiritual indwelling is described in this way: "That you may be strengthened through the Spirit, so that Christ may dwell in your hearts by faith, rooted in love, etc." Thus the ancients say that Christ does not only dwell in us in this spiritual manner, but that in the Supper the body and blood of Christ are communicated to us in such a way that He dwells in us bodily, naturally, and fleshly. And they use this analogy, as when melted wax is not only worked into other wax by heat and by efficacy, but is actually mingled together with it. These are certainly very clear testimonies of the ancients.

The Zwinglians feel hard pressed by the perspicuity of these statements. Therefore, they also fabricate various ways of escape. Some say that the understanding of the Fathers is that Christ dwells in us bodily, but only in that He has assumed our nature. But without adding anything else, let a person consider simply this, that the Fathers manifestly say that Christ is united with us bodily in the use of the Supper, by the communion of His flesh, where there is certainly no incarnation taking place. And Hilary distinctly says both things: "We are in Christ through His bodily nativity, and He, in turn, is believed to be in us through the mystery of the Sacraments."

Others try to evade the instances where the Fathers affirm that Christ is joined together with us bodily in the reception of the Supper. This, they claim, is what the Fathers mean: That not only is the soul made alive from the spiritual communion of the vigor of the absent body of Christ, but our bodies also experience their own renewal from it. But it is entirely clear that the ancients, with the term "bodily," are not only looking at our bodies, but chiefly at the person of Christ, that He joins Himself to us not only with His spirit, that is, with His divinity, but also with His body, and that He does this not only effectively, but "by natural participation," as Cyril puts it. Therefore Chrysostom says that Christ joins Himself to us "with His body," while Hilary says, "with the flesh." These testimonies of the ancients, then, are manifest and firm against all sophistries.

Second. The ancients' understanding of the Lord's Supper cannot be understood any better than from those passages where, in the weightiest articles of faith, they draw their arguments from the doctrine of the Lord's Supper, especially against the keenest of heretics. As Irenaeus says, "Our understanding of the Eucharist is unanimous, and the Eucharist, in turn, confirms our understanding." But it is clear, as we will demonstrate, that in those argumentations, it makes no sense—indeed, it is plainly contradictory—if we are to understand the communion of an absent body, either by symbolism or by efficacy alone.

The Arians imagined that the Father is in the Son, not because of the same substance (ὁμοούσιον), but because He is effective and works in Him. As their proof passage, they adduced the saying from John 17, "I in them, You in Me, etc." This is how they formed their argument: Christ is in believers only with regard to vigor and efficacy, not substance; therefore, this is how the Father is in the Son. Hilary refutes this from the doctrine of the Lord's Supper, in this way: "In the use of the Supper, Christ is in us, not only with regard to vigor and efficacy, but bodily, naturally, and with the flesh. For through the Sacrament of His communicated flesh and blood, we have acquired the nature of His flesh." Similarly: "When we have received and consumed these things, they have this effect, that we are in Christ, and Christ in us. Therefore also the unity between Father and Son is not only to be understood with regard to obedience and will, but naturally, etc." If we were to substitute here either the sign or the efficacy of an absent body, then the Arians have surely won, and Hilary is merely arguing against himself.

Third. Apollinaris and Eutyches, who imagined that in the incarnate Christ, after the union, there are not and do not remain two distinct and integral natures, were refuted in this way by Chrysostom, Gelasius, and others, from the doctrine of the Lord's Supper: "Just as the Eucharist consists of two things, an earthly (bread and wine) and a heavenly (the body and blood of Christ), and those two things constitute one Sacrament, so in Christ, after the union, there are and remain two distinct and integral natures. There is no need either to remove the other nature, or to deny that He is one person." The ancient writer Justin also uses this analogy. But it is entirely clear that the opinion of Eutyches is not refuted, but aided if one suggests that the body of Christ is present in the Supper only with regard to power and efficacy, but not with the presence of the substance. These conclusions are utterly inescapable. Moreover, it is well-known what the Fathers' reasoning was behind these analogies, for the union between us and Christ is not like the oneness of the Father and the Son, nor is the union of bread and body in the Supper a personal union, as the two natures are united in the person of Christ. The ancients explain these things very clearly.

Fourth. In his epistle of the Council of Ephesus, Cyril argues thus: "It is written, 'Take. This is My body. This is My blood.' Therefore, if Christ were any man other than Christ the God-Man, we would receive only flesh, without the divinity, and thus it would be common flesh, which cannot give life. But since Christ professed that His flesh gives life, therefore it has been joined together with the Word, which, by nature, is life. Therefore, when we receive His body, we receive that flesh with which the divinity has been inseparably united. He is, therefore, one Person, etc." This argument cannot stand if the substance of Christ's body is removed from the Supper, if a person pretends that we only receive His spirit, that is, His divinity.

Fifth. Irenaeus drew from the doctrine of the Lord's Supper the argument that Christ assumed true flesh and that it was true blood that was shed for us. He adds, "The blood is none other than the blood that comes from veins and flesh and from the remaining substance which is according to man." This is what the ancients say, that Christ provided the Apostles with a certain argument of His resurrection, namely, that His flesh would not remain in death nor would it see corruption, for He says, "Take; eat. This is My body.

Drink. This is My blood." And Cyril also says, "If the flesh of Christ restored corrupted things by His touch alone, how will our corruptible flesh not be restored to life, since it is joined to that flesh which has become life, the flesh which we taste and eat." Irenaeus makes the same argument on several occasions with many words, as does Justin. But these arguments would be entirely futile if the true and substantial presence and distribution of the body and blood of the Lord were removed from the Supper. All this is clear.

Sixth. We should also consider those sayings which frequently occur among the ancients from which their understanding can be clearly determined; namely, how the body and blood of the Lord are received in the Eucharist. For they say that it is done "not only by faith in the soul, but with the body and the mouth, etc." Irenaeus says, "Our bodies receive the Eucharist, which consists of two things." In commenting on the holy kiss in the last chapter of 2 Corinthians, "He has entered through these doors and gates. Indeed, Christ daily enters us when we commune (you who are partakers of the mysteries know what this means). Yes, our mouth has obtained an uncommon honor, receiving the body of the Lord. This is where the holy kiss comes from." And he says in Homily 60, "The very blood of Christ is in the mysteries, and in the reception He names hands, mouth, tongue, etc."

Ambrose says to Theodosius in *Historia Tripartita,* Book 9, ch. 30, "How will you receive the sacrosanct body of the Lord with hands of this kind? How will you approach that precious blood with your mouth?" Augustine, Epistle 118, "It pleased the Holy Spirit, in honor of such a great Sacrament, that the Lord's body should enter the mouth of the Christian before other foods." He says the same thing in *Contra Adversarium Legis,* Bk. 2, ch. 9, that it is received "by the believing heart and mouth." *De Consecr.*, dist. 2, the statement of Gregory is cited: "You have learned what the blood of the Lamb is, not by hearing, but by drinking. This blood is placed over both doorposts when it is consumed not only with the mouth of the body, but also with the mouth of the heart." And Leo, Sermon 6, *De Ieiunio*: "That which is believed with the heart is there received with the mouth." And Chrysostom exclaims, "This is a great miracle!" But there would be no need of a great miracle if the mouth received only plain bread.

Finally. This observation is also worth considering, that although dissimilar statements from the Fathers may be accumulated, nevertheless the negative statement is clearly nowhere to be found, although the affirmative is repeated many times. They cite Chrysostom on Matthew 5: "The true body of Christ is not in the holy vessels; only the mystery of it is contained therein." But this citation shows that, although they search every page of the Fathers anxiously and zealously, they are unable to find the negative in the Fathers. For the statement cited above is found in an incomplete work which they know very well does not belong to Chrysostom. Nor are they unaware that Erasmus has noted many things in that work which cannot be credibly proved. For in it the equality of the Father and the Son is denied; the Homoousians are listed among the heretics; the Holy Spirit is described as being less than the Son and as His servant; remarriage is condemned, etc. What authority, then, would this testimony have, even if it entirely denied the presence of Christ's body in the Supper? But it does not even do that! It speaks of the sacred vessels of the Old Testament, which Balthasar profaned (Daniel 5), and does not mention the Lord's Supper with even a single word. Let the passage merely be inspected. Berengarius long ago cited a statement from Augustine on the 98th Psalm: "Not this body which it seems you are about to eat, etc." But in that passage, Augustine expressly says in the preceding words, "He received flesh from the flesh of Mary, and in that very flesh He walked, and that very flesh He has given us to eat for our salvation." Therefore, he simply rejects the Capernaitic eating.

This is a very solid argument: that no negative statement can be clearly demonstrated in any of the Fathers' writings. Thus when Chrysostom treats the doctrine of the Lord's Supper, he mentions the article of the ascension to heaven. But he does not conclude from that the absence of the body of Christ in the Supper. He says, "Let us consider that we are tasting the One who sits above, who is adored by angels." Likewise, he brings up the passage, "The poor you have with you always, but Me you do not always have." But he only responds with the second statement, "Behold, I am with you until the end of the age, etc." These observations clearly and definitively demonstrate, against all sophistries, what the ancient and purer Church thought about the Lord's Supper, and in my opinion, they bring more light and usefulness than if great numbers of dissimilar statements were accumulated, etc. Moreover, I have not included here the whole passages, since many others have already compiled them.

XVIII. Modes of speaking.

In all topics of Christian doctrine, it is customary, after the true understanding has been established, to include some reminders about modes of speaking. For due to the petulance of clever men, debates over expressions often cause more trouble than the matters themselves. Indeed, insidious disputations are generally stirred up intentionally concerning modes of speaking, so that, through these subterfuges, a safer and less offensive method for undermining the matters themselves may be furnished for the majority, who think that the conflict is not about the matters at hand, but only about the words, as in this controversy. There are very many examples of this kind. Therefore, after we have learned from the Word of God what the correct faith is concerning the Lord's Supper, it is useful for us also to learn to understand the true foundations of the modes of speaking; and, as we wish to think piously, that we also learn to speak reverently about these great mysteries; and due to the treachery of the adversaries, that we may know in what sense and for which reasons some modes of speaking have been used for the sake of teaching, for a more suitable clarification of our faith.

But here at the beginning, without any doubt the best and most suitable modes of speaking in this doctrine are those which the Son of God Himself used in the institution and which the Apostles later used in the repetition of this doctrine. Holding out the bread, He says, "This (which is being given, which you are receiving) is My body. This cup is the New Testament in My blood. The cup of the Lord is the blood of Christ, which is of the New Testament, etc. The bread which we break in the Supper is the communion of the body of Christ, which was given for you." These are the words of Scripture. Luther says that he often tested whether the understanding of the true presence and distribution of the body and blood of the Lord in the Supper could be set forth with more proper and suitable words. But he says that he found that it cannot be described any more meaningfully than with the words, "This is My body, etc." So, then, as for those who do not want to speak of this proposition, that the bread and wine of the Lord's Supper are the true body and the true blood of Christ, it is for them to decide. For, by the same rationale, the words of Christ in the institution will also be rejected. But whatever may be or may be done concerning the rest of the modes of speaking, it is certain that the one which the Son of God used must be chiefly employed, retained, and defended.

But then these formulas have been used and received, that the body and blood of Christ are present with the bread, in the bread, under the bread, and that they are given to those who eat and drink. But here they object, "How can you speak like this, if one is not to depart from the words of Christ?" Yes, the godly who have not been fortified beforehand can be troubled by those objections. "Why do we use other manners of speaking? Why do we not simply retain the pattern of Christ's words? Surely we should not think that we can speak more suitably about those mysteries than the Son of God spoke when He instituted this Sacrament!"

We must consider, therefore, by what authority and for which reasons these formulas have been received, for then we will understand the use of them more correctly and will love them all the more. We will also know when we should fight for them and when not. For Luther rightly says that there is a great difference between these modes of speaking and that other formula which the Son of God used. For Christ's formula must at no time, in no way, and for no reason be rejected or omitted. But concerning the rest, Luther rightly says that, if they were to become an obstacle to the soundness of faith and upset the consensus on the true understanding, then we should be willing to abandon them entirely and retain that formula which the Son of God used.

Nevertheless, those other formulas have not been received entirely without the authority of Scripture. For when Paul says, "The bread which we break is the communion of the body of Christ," he clearly shows that two things are at once present and given and are to be included together in our speaking, as we said above about the sacramental predication and synecdoche. For these formulas—with the bread, in the bread, under the bread, etc.—are drawn and are rightly understood from that foundation. And there are genuine and serious reasons why we use those phrases more frequently, namely (as Augustine says about the terms "essence" and "person"), against the traps and errors of the heretics, so that, in the confession of our faith, we may be able to expressly make clear from whose false opinions we dissent, and so that we may be able to remove the disguise from the dishonest adversaries.

For example, the Papists imagine, apart from Scripture, that the substance of the bread is annihilated and converted or transubstantiated into the body of Christ. In order to make clear that we do not approve of that invention of transubstantiation, but believe and confess with the ancient and purer Church that the Eucharist consists of two things, we say that the body of Christ is present, given, and received with the bread.

Likewise, the Sacramentarians continually lay that infamously false charge on us, as if we suggested a personal union of bread and body. Therefore, we expressly make our opposition clear when we say that the body and blood of *Christ* are present and given with the bread and with the wine. For we do not speak of the personal union in that way, asserting that God is present with that Man. But we suitably speak in this way about the sacramental union, which we call a true and substantial presence.

Furthermore, since the Zwinglians elude that formula ("with the bread") in this way, "as an absent house is handed over with a key, etc.," such a mode of speaking had to be sought which could not be so easily eluded, but which expressly and meaningfully showed that we do not believe and confess the sign, symbol, vigor, or efficacy of an absent body, etc., but the true and substantial presence of the body and blood of Christ in the Lord's Supper. Therefore, when we say, "in the bread," we do not refer to a local inclusion, but we say it in order to rule out any idea of the absence of the substance of the body and blood of Christ and to describe the true presence and distribution. But since this is not done visibly or according to the senses, our people have said, together with antiquity, "under the bread and under the wine, etc."

Therefore, the rule which should guide the modes of speaking in this topic is this: We should, without any ambiguity, expressly declare the genuine understanding in such a way that we testify that we disagree with the Transubstantiators and with all those who deny the true presence of the body and blood of the Lord in the Supper. This makes those appeasements all the more insidious in which such high, poetic modes of speaking are set forth under which the Zwinglians can easily hide their errors and thus spread their poison among the unwary. We, however, use these modes of speaking indifferently, in order to clarify that we simply believe the words of institution concerning the presence of the body and blood of the Lord. But with regard to the mode of presence, we should not inquire into it speculatively, but should commend it to God's omnipotence. Therefore, those modes of speaking have been received with genuine authority and for the most serious of reasons. And yet they have not first been devised during these past thirty years; purer antiquity itself spoke in this way long before these Sacramentarian conflicts arose.

Chrysostom says on that statement which was cited above, "Under sensory things and in sensory things."

Augustine says, *De Sententiis Prosperi*: "We drink His blood under the appearance and taste of wine."

He says the same thing, *Ad Neophyt.*: "Take, in the bread, that which hung on the tree. Take, in the cup, that which was poured out from Christ's side."

Cyril, in his Epistle *Ad Calosyrium,*: "We receive in the bread and wine His sacred flesh and His precious blood in a life-giving benediction."

Augustine, *De Catechisandis Rudibus*, ch. 26, says: "Invisible things are honored in visible seals."

Hesychius on chapter 8 of Leviticus: "That mystery is at once bread and flesh."

Chrysostom on the passage, "The cup which we bless, etc.": "Yes, with the cup we approach the indescribable benefits of God and whatever things we have obtained."

So also the Scripture says in Exodus 14: "The angel of the Lord who went before the camp moved and went behind them, and with him a pillar of cloud."

Likewise in Exodus 3: "The Lord appeared to him in a flame of fire." Numbers 12: "The Lord descended in a pillar of cloud."

And yet in these examples, a true presence, not a local inclusion, is signified.

Furthermore, something must be said about those adverbs, *truly, bodily, substantially, really,* etc., which are often added. For some people prattle that those words are exotic, alien, and entirely foreign to the phraseology of Scripture, first invented by scholastic writers. Therefore, we must see, **first**, who the first authors were who used those terms; **second**, for what purpose and for which reasons those adverbs are normally added. The fact is, these terms are found among the most ancient and approved writers, and indeed, in their very disputations about the Lord's Supper. For Hilary, *De Trinitate*, ch. 8, speaking about how the Eucharist is the communion of the flesh and blood of Christ, repeatedly uses these formulas: *truly, naturally, bodily, through flesh*. But Hilary did not mean that the body was present and distributed in a bodily, natural, visible, sensory way, for he calls it a "Mystery" and a "Sacrament." No, this is all he meant to signify: that the very substance and nature of the body and blood of Christ is present, distributed, and received, not as a sign, nor according to efficacy only, but *truly*.

Cyril, Bk. 10, ch. 13 on John, speaking of the communion of the body and blood of Christ in the Eucharist, often repeats "the bodily union, the natural participation." And lest there be any ambiguity, he makes such an antithesis, not only spiritually, but also bodily. Likewise, "Not only according to the spirit, but also according to the flesh."

Similarly, in Bk. 11, ch. 27, he combines both things, bodily and substantially. "For receiving bodily and substantially (as we have said) the Son of God, who is united by nature with the Father, etc." Chrysostom says, "He mingles Himself with us through His body in that food of which He says, 'Take, eat.'" As Hilary says, "through His flesh."

Again, Chrysostom says, "Not only by faith and spiritually, but *re ipsa*, by the thing itself." And Cyril says, "*Re vera*, by the true thing."

From there, Paschasius and those who later opposed Berengarius adopted the adverb "*realiter*, really."

Augustine often uses the adverb "invisibly," as in Psalm 98, In *Sententiis Prosperi, De Catechisandis Rudibus*, etc. For the sake of brevity, I will not include here the full statements, since they are well-known from the writings of many.

These observations should be considered for the sake of those who write such decrees by their own dictatorial authority: "We say that the body of Christ is given efficaciously in the Lord's Supper, not naturally, that it is given according to power, not according to substance, etc." But the whole of antiquity not only disagrees with this, but also speaks against it outright. "Not only efficaciously, but naturally; not according to power only, but substantially, bodily, etc."

Now we must also see for what purpose and for which reasons those adverbs are normally added to the confessions about the Lord's Supper.

It is well-known, moreover, that in the first heat of contention, it was claimed that the bread is only Christ's body according to sign and symbol. On this point, our theologians thought it sufficient to answer with that adverb with which Hilary had previously described the truth of the presence of the body and blood of the Lord, namely, that the body and blood of the Lord are *truly* present and given with the bread and wine, just as the Apostles say of the resurrection of Christ in Luke 24, "The Lord has *truly* risen."

But afterwards, the Zwinglians began to moderate their own expressions, seeing that the ears of the pious were offended by them. They said that, yes, the *true* body is present, but it is only present *spiritually*. And since the spiritual eating is not something fictitious or imaginary, they began to speak as we do, saying that the true body is *truly* present. But they understood it, not according to the substance of the body, but only spiritually, that is, by the contemplation of faith and effectively. For they use this example: Isaiah says, "This people is truly grass." There the adverb "truly" was added, and yet it is very clearly a metaphor. And thus through expressions that have "the appearance of truth" (as Nazianzus says), they spread their venom stealthily among the unwary, who suspected no evil, since they were hearing the same words, that the *true* body is *truly* present and given. Therefore, in order to draw out the hidden adversaries with their dangerous snares, lest they be able to inflict their ambiguous expressions on the unskilled, our theologians, compelled by necessity, added those terms which had been used by the ancients for the same reason, namely, "substantially, bodily, really, etc."

For those terms cannot so easily be eluded with insidious interpretation. They furnish a norm according to which simpler people can discern the voice of the true Shepherd from the howling wolves who imitate the bleating of sheep. However, the mode of presence is not described with these terms, but only as with the ancients, they signify that the body of Christ is present in the Supper and given to those who eat and drink, not only according to power and efficacy, but also according to substance. For the body which was given for us is certainly not in the category of a quality or rhetorical figure, but in the category of a substance.

This observation, too, is useful, that the ancients reject those same adverbs when they are taken and explained concerning the natural and carnal mode of presence. For Paschasius says on several occasions that the body of Christ is not present carnally in the Supper, that is, not in a natural, but in a supernatural and heavenly way. Thus Augustine says on many occasions that Christ is not present with us now with a bodily presence, that is, (as he himself explains in Treatise 64 on John), "not in a bodily, visible, palpable way, etc., as He walked on the earth prior to His suffering, or as He caused Himself to be seen up until His ascension, and as He will be at the judgment." So also he says in Sermon 177, "He abandoned His disciples in His bodily form, etc."

I add this, because the adversaries play an insidious game with these equivocations. Thus far on modes of speaking.

XIX. The recitation of the words of institution, which they commonly call "the consecration."

Many things have been said among the scholastics about this disputed topic. Some of them are useless, and some are also superstitious. There is no reason to recite those. There is a book by Bessarion in which he disputes at length the question of whether the consecration is done through the words of the Canon, or through the words of institution. The Papists also imagined at one time that it was through the Canon, and they still defend that position today: That, after the words of consecration have been recited, an indivisible joining together of body and bread is made in an absolute sense; that is, even apart from the use, if there is no one to take and eat. But that is the same as if someone recited the words of Baptism over water with no one present to be baptized. For that perpetual and immovable rule must remain: The Sacraments do not have the nature of a Sacrament apart from the use for which they were instituted.

On the other hand, some rejected the consecration in such a way that they thought that the Supper could be celebrated even without the words of institution. But it is most certain that, if the Word of God which is proper to each Sacrament is removed from the action, it is not a Sacrament, as Augustine rightly says. "Let the word be added to the element, and it becomes a Sacrament." By the same token, "Remove the Word, and what will the water be but water?" But the institution is the Word that is proper to this Sacrament. Therefore, if the Word is removed from it, it will certainly not be a true Sacrament. Pomeranus says, "It would be foolish to omit the words of Christ's institution, wicked not to trust in them. For without them, what, I ask, would we seek in the bread and in the cup?" Likewise, "Christ commanded us to do what He did. But He was not silent; He said, etc." And Paul expressly says that we "bless" ("the cup of blessing which we bless"), and no one should invent a special blessing for himself. Therefore, in the celebration of the Supper there must be a recitation of the words of Christ. But that recitation of the institution is not done like magicians who recite their incantations about Jupiter Elicius. Nor is it like the Papists who make up a story about a certain shepherd who was walking about among his sheep and was singing the words of consecration, which he had heard recited at some time but did not understand (even as men of this kind are accustomed to remembering the melodies that they sing, although they do not retain the words, and surely not the sense). But after he had, either by chance or on purpose, laid down his shepherd's sack, packed with bread, on a certain stone that was lying nearby, they imagine that at this recitation of the words, the bread in the sack was visibly changed into flesh. Others imagine an even greater miracle. But these are actually magical things.

But since Doctor Pomeranus has carefully, truly, and piously explained this question, I will submit his words. "We are not the ones who turn the bread into the body of Christ and the wine into His blood; we repeat the whole institution of Christ over the bread and the cup, as the privilege of our Prince, as the institution and ordination of Christ which will endure among the faithful until the end of the world. For when we come together, we do not here wish to eat normal bread or to drink a normal cup, but that bread and that cup which Christ instituted to be eaten and drunk in remembrance of Him. This bread and this cup were formerly normal bread and a normal cup. But when it comes to the institution of Christ, so that, coming together, we eat and drink in remembrance of Christ, now it is not normal bread and a normal cup, but it is the Lord's bread and the Lord's cup, not in the same way as the earth is the Lord's, but in a unique way, so that whoever eats this bread in an unworthy manner becomes guilty of the Lord's body." Likewise,

"Christ with His Word cannot be lacking in this institution, even as it is Christ who baptizes us, although He does it through the minister. So also He Himself gives us His body and blood in this Supper, although He does it through the minister. For when the words, 'Take, eat; this is My body,' are uttered, it is not the voice of the minister as a man. Therefore, it is certain that Christ Himself is present here and gives us His body and blood, causing the bread to be His body and the cup to be His blood by the Word of His institution. So it is that, although we visibly receive Christ's body and His blood through the hand of the minister, nevertheless we receive it invisibly from the hand of Christ by virtue and efficacy of the institution, that is, of His Word. Did He not promise? 'Where two or three are gathered together in My name, there will I be in their midst.' Therefore, He is there when we come together at His institution, and He gives us His body and blood, thus preserving His institution and the truth of His Word. For 'this is My body' is not our word, but the Word of Him who created all things and did all that He wanted by His omnipotent Word."

Likewise: "As for us, we repeat Christ's institution over the bread and wine, which have been taken up for this sacred use, in the presence of those who will commune, so that, on the basis of the words of Christ, they may hear and understand what they are to do and believe here. Christ says, 'Do this,' that is, 'Take the bread and eat My body, believing that the bread which you eat according to My institution, in remembrance of Me, is not simply bread, but My body, which is given for you, etc."

These are the words of Pomeranus taken from here and there in his little book. I have included as much as seemed necessary for our purpose, since I consider this to be the simplest understanding.

They commonly call "consecration" what Paul calls "blessing," a word taken from Mark's description, "the cup of blessing which we bless, etc." For this reason, Cyril almost always calls it a "mystic blessing." But whichever word is used, the question is this: From where, and by what power, does it happen that the body and blood of Christ are present, distributed, and received with the bread and wine in the Lord's Supper? It is clear from the most ancient writers that the recitation of the institution has always accompanied the administration of the Supper. (To say nothing of the rest, such as Chrysostom, Ambrose, and Augustine, who deal with that question as if by profession.) Justin says this: "We have been taught that the food which, through the prayer of the Word, is consecrated by the thanksgiving, is the flesh and blood of the incarnate Jesus Himself." But Irenaeus says most elegantly, "When the mixed cup and the broken bread perceive the Word of God, it becomes the Eucharist of the body and blood of Christ." And in another place he says something even more significant: "When the bread, which is of the earth, perceives the call of God, it is no longer normal bread, but the Eucharist, consisting of two things, etc." And this is a lovely saying: "When Christ calls the bread 'His body,' when He names the wine 'His blood,' then it is no longer normal bread, etc."

Dionysius also writes, "When the priest begins the administration of the Supper, he usually begins with the exclamation, 'How awesome it is that here we wish to distribute and receive the body and blood of Christ! But You have said, Do this, etc.'" In a matter so clear, I do not wish to add more.

XX. The eating on the part of the unworthy.

What do those who eat unworthily receive? This is not an idle question; it reveals something very important, namely, that the supreme mystery of the presence and reception of the body of Christ does not depend on worthiness or merit, either on the part of the one who gives or the one who receives, but solely on the ordinance and institution of the Son of God. For otherwise, there would be a perpetual and horrible doubt whether we are truly receiving the body of Christ, since we are forced to acknowledge that we are, in many ways, unworthy. This is why Christ wanted to make this institution so certain and sure for His Church, as Pomeranus says, "He lets even His wicked disciples eat His body and drink His blood, lest we should doubt that we, who observe the institution by true faith, truly and substantially receive the body and blood of Christ."

Secondly, this doctrine stirs up serious exercises of repentance and faith in the reception, for it is not simply bread, so that you may treat it more irreverently, but it is the body of the Lord, because of which you incur horrendous guilt if you approach it without repentance and faith. Thus Paul draws the most serious warnings from this in 1 Corinthians 11.

Finally, this question is the most dependable "criterion," as Luther says, by which the two-tongued and evasive Zwinglians can be drawn out into the light. For they have learned cleverly to force nearly all the other forms of speaking into their spiritual eating of an absent body. That is why I say these things, because this question is considered by many to be both idle and useless.

Now, to be clear, the question here is not about a mouse gnawing on the bread, nor about Turks, Jews, and others who are manifestly outside of the Christian religion. For Christ gave His Supper to His disciples, among whom also was Judas, by external profession. And Paul says that "we who are many are one body, for we all partake of the one bread." He is speaking, then, of the external gathering of the visible Church, in which there are many who are not reborn, and yet who are in agreement by an external profession of faith. Indeed, if someone's wickedness is manifest and notorious, the ministers have the most severe command not to cast pearls to swine. This, then, is the question: When the institution of Christ is observed in the Church, and some unworthily receive and eat, what do they take and eat? And since it is certain that the merits of Christ are not applied to such people—in other words, that such people do not eat the flesh of Christ spiritually—the Zwinglians say that those who eat unworthily do not take the body of Christ at all, nor do they drink His blood, but only the external symbols: the bread and the wine.

But there are three irrefutable proofs that the unworthy also take and eat the body of the Lord.

First. Neither the faith of the one who administers, nor of those who receive, makes the Sacraments; the institution and words of the Lord make the Sacraments when they are used. Moreover, Christ does not say in the institution, "If a worthy person approaches, he will eat My body; if an unworthy person approaches, He will eat only bread." No, He simply says to those present, "Take; eat. This is My body." Therefore, He will not change the truth of His institution on account of the unworthiness or wickedness of those who receive it.

Second. At the first supper, Christ invited to the table, not only Peter, but also Judas the betrayer, as John testifies that Judas went out "after the supper was ended." And He says both to Peter and Judas alike, "Take; eat. This is My body." So Augustine says, *Contra Fulgentium Donatistam*: "Judas the betrayer received the good body of Christ, and Simon Magus received His good Baptism. But since they did not use in a good way that which was good, these bad men, by using them badly, were destroyed." And in Epistle 162: "The Lord Himself puts up with Judas—that devil, that thief, and His betrayer. He permits him to receive among the innocent disciples that which the faithful know to be our ransom price."

Third. Paul affirms that those who eat unworthily become guilty of the body and blood of the Lord. And he says that this is done because, when they eat that bread of which Christ says, "This is My body," they do not discern the Lord's body, but receive it as if it were only normal bread, or as the loaves of showbread were. Therefore, Augustine says, *De Baptismo contra Donatistas*, Bk. 5, ch. 8:

"The one who receives the Lord's Sacrament unworthily does not cause it to be a bad thing simply because he is a bad person, nor does he receive nothing, simply because he does not receive it for salvation. For the body of the Lord and the blood of the Lord were also given to those of whom the Apostle said, 'Whoever eats unworthily eats and drinks judgment on himself.'"

These things are clear and firm. But this argument moves many: "If the flesh of Christ, due to the personal union, has become life, as Cyril says, how can it exist in someone who is ungodly, and yet fail to make him alive?" But let these same people explain how the divinity itself, which, in its essence, fills heaven and earth, exists essentially in the demons themselves, and yet does not make them alive with eternal life. Now, it is certain that faith is that instrument by which the life of Christ dwells in us efficaciously. So it is that Christ was in Nazareth, according to the substance of His body, but due to their unbelief He was not able to do any miracle there (Mark 6, Mat. 13). So it is that when the woman (Mark 5, Luke 8), touches the hem of Christ's cloak, power goes out from Him. Yet although the soldiers and the servant of the high priest touched the very body of Christ in His Passion, such power did not go out from Him. For, "Your faith has saved you," Christ said to the woman. In the same way, the cause of judgment for those who eat unworthily is not in Christ, for His flesh is and remains life and salvation. But the impenitence and unbelief of those who receive it is the cause. But Christ, to whom the Father has given the judgment, will judge that abuse and insult to His body and blood. The philanthropy, then, of the Son of God is immeasurable and indescribable. He shows that He so seriously desires and seeks the salvation of all men, that even to those who eat unworthily He gives His body, with a serious admonition concerning how they should use it in a salutary way. But they add to their former sins even this most grievous offense: That they tread upon and insult the body and blood of the Lord, which have been both given and received. And Paul undoubtedly had the most serious reasons for wanting to speak in this way. Those who receive unworthily eat judgment on themselves, for even as Christ is life and salvation to those who believe, so He says in John 3 about those who disbelieve, "This is the judgment, that light has come into the world, etc." Likewise in John 5, "The Father has given all judgment to the Son." And in John 9, "For judgment I have come into this world, so that those who see may be made blind."

Moreover, this doctrine of the eating on the part of the unworthy should be rightly set forth, lest the more timid consciences be disturbed. For Paul does not say, "Whoever is unworthy of this great treasure eats judgment on himself." For we are all unworthy even of daily bread, and antiquity rightly applied here those words of the centurion, "Lord, I am not worthy for You to come under my roof." Nor should we think that a salutary eating depends on our worthiness, as the Papists teach that those who approach should prepare themselves in such a way—with proper works, merits, and satisfactions—that they are clean from sins, and thus become worthy of that heavenly food. But this is contrary to the purpose and use of this Sacrament, which was instituted for those who feel the sin dwelling in their flesh, who acknowledge and admit the imperfection of their repentance, the infirmity of their faith, and the uncleanness of their love. The healthy are not the ones who need the medicine, but those who acknowledge their disease in such a way that they desire to be healed. Therefore, unworthy eating is the unworthy use, and Ambrose describes it thus: "Whoever celebrates this mystery in another way and approaches it with another intention than what was given by the Lord, he eats unworthily."

Therefore, the doctrine of the true use of the Lord's Supper will reveal exactly what it means to eat unworthily. For the sake of brevity, we will note only the major headings. **First**, a person eats unworthily when the institution of Christ is not observed but is violated and twisted in those things which pertain to the substance of this Sacrament. **Second**, those who approach with irreligious thoughtlessness, so that they do not consider the magnitude of that mystery but treat it no more reverently than they treat bread in the common dining room. For Paul expressly notes this practice among the Corinthians. **Third**, those who approach without a serious recognition of their own filthiness, being puffed up with a confidence in their own righteousness. They do not seek there the forgiveness of sins and the healing of their infirmities, but approach as if they were worthy of that heavenly food. Such people eat in a truly unworthy manner. For Christ says, "given and shed for you for the forgiveness of sins," and, "it is the New Testament, etc." **Fourth**, those who, without repentance, continue in sins against conscience, whether internal or external; likewise, those who intend to go on sinning or to return to their sins. For Christ instituted this Sacrament so that we may seek release from sins. It is obviously diametrically opposed to seeking release from sin if someone is thinking about continuing in sin or embracing sin. **Fifth**, those who do not approach the reception of the Sacrament with a true faith which, with full confidence, applies to itself the merits of the death and resurrection of Christ; instead, they attribute this either to the reception itself—by simply doing the work—or to other works. **Sixth**, those who attach other purposes to this Sacrament, such as those who turn it into a propitiatory sacrifice, or who turn the Mass into some kind of necessary work, etc.

These things are plain, for just as those who use this Sacrament according to its genuine use eat worthily, so, on the other hand, unworthy eating is at odds with the genuine use.

XXI. The veneration of the Sacrament.

Right at the beginning, we must expressly address the bread-worship (ἀρτολατρεία) of the Papists. For when the bread is reserved in the pyx, or when it is carried around and put on display in processions, or treated in some way outside of the use instituted by Christ, it is certain that the institution is not being observed. The institution and words of Christ create the Sacraments when they are being used. Therefore, when the Sacrament is not there, and when the body of Christ is not present, it is a dreadful abuse and horrendous form of idolatry to give to the bread the honor which is due to God alone. Indeed, to gaze upon and to venerate the bread as it is carried around and put on display, apart from the Communion—with gold, candles, genuflections, etc., with the opinion that, by simply doing the work, those who persevere in transgressions, without repentance and faith, are helped thereby simply because they are spectators of the display, of the carrying around, or of the histrionic representation in the Mass—is something far worse than hypocrisy. Yes, these idolatrous abuses must be severely censured.

But when Luther, *Contra Lovanienses,* Art. 16, calls the Eucharist a "venerable and adorable Sacrament," he means when the institution of Christ is being observed and the Sacrament is being used. For if we truly believe that Jesus Christ, the Son of God, is present in that action with a special mode of presence, so that there He truly and substantially gives to the participants His body and blood by which He wants to join Himself with us in such a way that each one of the recipients applies to himself by faith the gifts of the New Testament which Christ acquired by the giving of His body and the shedding of His blood—if, I say, we believe this with all our heart and mind, then the question about the adoration and veneration of the Sacrament is plain. When, Jacob, in Genesis 28, saw the Lord standing above the ladder, he had no special command to worship the Lord there. Nor did Moses in Exodus 34, or Elijah in 1 Kings 19. But since they believed that God was present there and was revealing Himself with a special mode of grace, it certainly would not have been a true faith if invocation or adoration had not followed. That is the honor which is due to God. But this warning must be added: The Sacrament is not to be worshiped in the same way as we venerate, with one adoration, the humanity and the divinity in the Person of Christ on account of the personal union. For the union of the bread and the body of Christ in the Supper is not like this. But since the Eucharist consists of two things, an earthly and a heavenly, the worship and veneration should not be directed at the earthly elements of bread and wine, but at Christ, God and Man, who has instituted and revealed His presence in that action with a special mode of grace, even as the Israelites, in the ark of the covenant, did not worship the wood or the gold or the Cherubim, but God, who had promised to be present there. And since, beyond controversy, true worship consists in thanksgiving, invocation, and confession, I think this is the simplest way to understand what should be concluded about the worship and veneration of the Sacrament if it is clarified according to these three parts.

First. The ancients called it the "Eucharist" because, while the immeasurable benefits of the Son of God are always to be pondered, considered, and celebrated with a grateful mind, it is especially so in this action, because not only was the Word made flesh for us, not only did He offer the body of His flesh and shed His blood on the cross for our redemption, but in addition to all this, He shares that body with us to be eaten and that blood to be drunk in this Sacrament, in order that He may thus, with a most certain pledge, apply the New Testament to each recipient individually, and in order that, by means of a very brief covenant, He may join Himself to this wretched clay of ours and also prepare our body for the resurrection and immortality, etc. If this Eucharist is lacking, there can certainly be no worthy eating. For what else does it mean, I ask, when Christ says, "This do in remembrance of Me," which Paul explains, "You will announce the Lord's death, etc."? Indeed, this is, without a doubt, a part of genuine worship.

Second. When true faith is present, it cannot happen that the one who approaches the Supper, considering the greatness of the mystery, should eat judgment on himself by an unworthy reception, even as he, with ardent prayers, calls upon Christ the God-

Man, whom he believes to be truly and substantially present in that action, that he may not, by unworthy eating, become guilty, but rather that he be grafted into His most holy body and His precious blood, that he may draw life from it, as the branches from the vine, for the preservation of faith, for the mortification of the body of sin, for the increase in love, etc., as we said more fully above concerning the salutary use of this Supper. We certainly pray for these things publicly in the action of this Supper with solemn prayers. It pertains, likewise, to the exercise of true faith, that in serious repentance, the recipient, considering the magnitude of his filthiness, seriously asks that he be received and preserved in that covenant of the New Testament by which God, for the sake of the body of Christ which was given for us and the blood which was shed for us, wants to be favorable toward believers with regard to their sins and not to remember their iniquity any longer. Likewise, since faith is necessary, if we rightly consider how faint its beginnings are in us, then we will, with genuine sighing, implore the Author and Perfecter of our faith (Hebrews 12), "Lord, I believe. But You Yourself, bring aid for my unbelief!" Likewise, "Increase our faith!" Indeed, this invocation is certainly the chief and foremost part of true worship.

But the following pertains to the **third** part of worship, namely, confession. When Paul says that, in the reception, one must discern the body of the Lord, he clearly teaches, as Ambrose says, that one must approach with fear, so that the mind knows that it owes reverence toward Him whose body he is going to receive, for he should discern within himself that it is the Lord whose blood he is drinking in this mystery. For this reason, Chrysostom calls them, "fearful mysteries" and "a fearful cup." Likewise, he says, "Let us consider that we are tasting Him who sits on high, who is worshiped by angels, etc." These things are certainly true, if we believe that Christ is truly present in that action and gives His body and blood to those who eat and drink.

Indeed, this is the true worship and veneration of this Sacrament, for this inner veneration in the heart must surely come first, or else the outer reverence is mere hypocrisy. But when the heart on the inside feels this way about this Sacrament and approaches with this devotion, as we have said, then the external actions follow willingly and spontaneously in reverence and veneration of this Sacrament. Indeed, these should be an external confession of what we understand and believe about this Supper, so that, by public confession, we distinguish ourselves from those who deny the true presence of the body and blood of the Lord in the Supper, and so that we may not give occasion to the simpler people for profane ideas, or give to the swine the opportunity to trample these venerable mysteries. For outward irreverence is a sign of a profane mind, as Paul says that the Corinthians did not distinguish the body of the Lord, since they treated the Lord's Supper with no more reverence than their common dining room. But concerning this external veneration of the Sacrament, I will note here a passage from Luther, who says, in commenting on Genesis 47, "As for us, we should bend the knee, or at least stand, not only when we pray, but also when we baptize, when we absolve, when we are absolved, and when we approach the holy Synaxis, yes, even at the recitation of the promise or of the Gospel text, as a sign of worship, that is, of reverence and gratitude. Therefore, even if nothing else were being offered in the Lord's Supper besides bread and wine (as the Sacramentarians blaspheme), the divine voice and the promise and the Holy Spirit are there through the Word in the Supper, and for that reason it would be fitting for us to approach with reverence. But how much more fitting it is, since we believe that Christ's true body and true blood are present together with the word!" Thus far Luther.

But in this whole business of the veneration of the Sacrament, it is useful to observe the rule which Ambrose taught on 1 Corinthians 11: "To the Lord it is unworthy when a person celebrates the mystery differently than it was given by Him. For he cannot be devout who thinks of it differently than it was given by its Author. Therefore, according to the given order, let the mind of the one who approaches the Eucharist be devout, etc." This rule is necessary so that no one imagines for himself a peculiar devotion and veneration of this Sacrament.

XXII. The arguments of the adversaries.

Now that the genuine understanding has been established from the proper, clear, and firm foundations of God's Word and has been reasonably clarified, something must now finally be said about the chief arguments of the Zwinglians with which they strive to upset and to shatter this simple and well-founded faith, lest any vestige should be left which might disturb the firm and certain assurance of the conscience. For they clamor that an infinite number of legal and logical contradictions of many articles of faith come about, if the understanding which we have affirmed thus far is accepted. Indeed, at the beginning of this controversy, the Zwinglians employed hundreds of arguments; there is a published book which sets forth 300 of them. This is what they learned in the rhetoric schools, as Quintilian says, "Arguments which are naturally weak are sustained by mutual aid. Therefore, if they cannot stand because they are good, they will stand because they are many." On the other hand, "The speech of truth is simple" (Seneca, Ep. 49). As Pindarus says, "For a righteous cause, three words will suffice."

But now many axioms which were initially considered by them to be a bronze wall are partly passed over in silence and partly rejected outright. For without any argument they reject Carlstadt's foolish fabrication about the disagreement of the demonstrative pronoun τοῦτο, "this," with the preceding noun ἄρτος, "bread." For they see that, in the Greek language, it is customary that the demonstrative pronouns correspond with the gender of the noun that follows, even when they clearly point to that which precedes, as in Genesis 2, when God formed the woman from Adam's rib, "He brought her to Adam, and Adam said, 'This (τοῦτο) is now bone of my bones.'" Here "woman" is feminine, but "this" (τοῦτο) is neuter, and yet it is clear what the demonstrative is pointing to. And where Matthew had said, τοῦτο τὸ αἷμά μου, "This is My blood," Luke adds, Τοῦτο τὸ ποτήριον, "This cup," for the sake of clarification, lest it be left ambiguous to what the demonstrative τοῦτο was referring. And when Paul says, "The bread which we break is the communion of the body of Christ," the demonstrative "this" clearly refers to the bread which is distributed.

Similarly, what they previously affirmed with a loud voice—that after Christ said, *"It is finished," His flesh, having plainly fulfilled its service, accomplished all the things for which it had been assumed, so that it now does nothing in the matter of vivification*—this they now expressly reject, namely, the idea that the flesh of Christ is not beneficial for vivification, that this is done by His divinity alone. These statements are no longer heard: "*That which is born of flesh is flesh. We have not known Christ according to the flesh.*" "*The Holy Spirit confirms faith, seals the righteousness of faith. Therefore, the Sacraments are merely signs of external profession.*" Now one hardly hears the softest whispers of that argument in which Carlstadt used to place his last hope of victory, based on Matthew 24: "*If anyone says to you, 'Behold, here is the Christ! Or there!,' do not believe it. For false prophets will arise, etc.*" *Therefore, those who teach that Christ is present in His Supper are false prophets, and Christ says, "Do not believe!"* Likewise, what they previously wanted to be held up on display, they now only mention briefly in passing, as if they have something better to do, namely, that passage from Colossians 3: *"Seek the things which are above, where Christ is sitting at God's right hand, not the things which are on the earth." "Therefore, in the Lord's Supper, which is celebrated on the earth, Christ is not present and is not to be sought."* This argument has also been muffled: *"In the Lord's Supper are the elements of bread and wine. But Paul says in Galatians 4, 'How are you turned again to weak and destitute elements?' Or in Colossians 2, 'That no one may deceive you according to the elements of the world, etc.'"* For they notice that these arguments not only suffer due to their weakness, but they also betray how uncertain are the foundations on which the Sacramentarian opinion depends. In fact, Luther rightly says that one can understand just how much certainty lies in the Sacramentarian opinion from the fact that the foundations themselves are so often changed.

Therefore, I will not comment on all their arguments, but only those which seem to be the most important to them and which have some appearance of soundness. I think, moreover, that it will be easiest, both for the sake of brevity and logical order, if arguments of the same kind are related to a single topic from which they have been drawn, as, for instance, to the article of the human nature in Christ, or of His ascension into heaven, etc. For thus the sources of their explanations can be more properly demonstrated, and there will be no need to repeat the same things over and over again.

XXIII. *The arguments of the Sacramentarians from the article of the human nature in Christ.*

"It is obvious that human bodies are circumscribed in a single, definite place in such a way that they cannot substantially be in many different places at one and the same time. Therefore, since the body which the Son of God assumed is of one substance (*consubstantiale*) with us, as the Council of Chalcedon says, it cannot be substantially present at one and the same time in heaven and in all those places where the Lord's Supper is celebrated according to His institution."

Here they insist with many words that they have not drawn this argument from notions of geometry or the principles of physics, but from the Word of God, which manifestly affirms this.

Hebrews 2: "In all things He had to be made like His brothers, except for sin." Romans 8: "In the likeness of the flesh of sin." Philippians 2: "He was made in the likeness of men and in condition was found as a man." Likewise, the Scripture testifies that the union of the two natures into one person of Christ was made without confusion or conversion, with the properties of each nature being preserved intact. Therefore, on account of the genuineness of the human nature in Christ, His body can only be in a single place, for otherwise He would not be in all things like His brothers, although Scripture affirms that He is.

ANSWER

I will not compose lengthy arguments, but I will simply and briefly note the main headings of the refutations which are found in the more copious explanations of other men. And since without any controversy the genuine explanation of this argument consists in the doctrine of the communion of properties (*communicatio idiomatum*), I have included a treatise at the end, where that doctrine has been sufficiently explained. Therefore, here I will be rather brief. The summary is as follows.

We confess and teach that the Son of God assumed a true human nature, with those properties which pertain to the condition of the human nature, and also with those infirmities with which our nature has been burdened on account of sin, so that He is like His brothers in all things, except for sin. We also add the doctrine of the reasons why He willingly also assumed those infirmities which do not have to do with the substance of human nature but have entered through sin. Therefore, we by no means remove from Christ the genuineness of the human nature.

But this is the question, this is the point at issue: Whether Christ, according to His human nature, is like His brothers in all things in such a way that, when Scripture predicates something of

His flesh which goes beyond the condition and attributes of our bodies, it is not to be conceded or believed, since Christ should be like His brothers in all things according to His human nature. Certainly "the blood of Christ purifies us from all sins" (1 John 1). "In His blood we have redemption" (Ephesians 1). "We have been justified in His blood" (Romans 5). "By His wounds we are healed" (Isaiah 53). "It is My flesh, which I will give for the life of the world" (John 6). "It was impossible for His flesh to see corruption" (Acts 2).

We believe these things about the flesh of Christ—things which cannot be attributed to our bodies without manifest idolatry—because Scripture affirms them, and we should believe them under peril of salvation. Therefore, we should not only press that single axiom from Hebrews 2 and 4, but we must combine both of these things, as Scripture does: **First**, that Christ, having assumed the properties and infirmities of our nature, was made like His brothers in all things, except for sin. **Second**, that on account of the personal union with the divinity, the human nature in Christ has many prerogatives which are alien to our bodies and which surpass the condition or attributes of our nature in infinite ways. And from this solid foundation, the force of the argument in which the Zwinglians place their chief hope of victory is cut off.

But we will not make our case about what is from what is possible, based solely on the consequence of the prerogatives of Christ's flesh, without the clear Word of God, as some have imagined concerning the union with the divinity, from argumentations alone, apart from and contrary to God's Word, that no true sense of pain could infect Christ's body, as rust cannot infect red-hot iron. But we begin from the clear Word of God. And when we read there that something is predicated of the human nature in Christ, we neither deny it nor elude it simply because we do not find such properties in the bodies of His brothers, but we believe what the Scripture affirms, because in that body alone dwells the entire divinity bodily.

The Evangelists tell how Christ walked with His body upon the waves of the sea so that He did not sink; how He vanished from their sight; how He suddenly stood in the midst while the doors were shut. These things are certainly not properties of our bodies, and yet He was made like His brothers in all things. Why, then, do we believe those things when the Evangelists say them?

Surely it is because of that axiom which Cyril puts in these words: "Since it is the very own body of the only-begotten God, it transcends all things human."

But in the Supper, it is not merely a historical recitation, but a serious affirmation of the Son of God Himself, who, while visibly reclining at table with His body in a physical location, says to His disciples, "That which you are each taking is My body." Likewise, after He had already received heaven, He delivered to Paul: "That which you distribute and receive in the Supper, wherever on earth the institution is observed, is My body." Therefore, since the Son of God Himself predicates and affirms this about His own body with express and entirely unambiguous words, as has been shown, we should certainly neither deny nor elude this simply because it is inconsistent with our bodies.

But since both things are true—that the flesh of Christ is like His brothers, and that, in addition to and beyond that likeness, He has many prerogatives which are in no way consistent with the bodies of His brothers—we should consider that the body of which the Son of God says, "This is My body; this is My blood," has very great prerogatives in this matter. For **first**, this body has the word, "Take, eat; this is My body." Now, if the word of Christ commanding Peter to come to Him upon the waters was able to create that difference, so that Peter walked upon the waves with the weight of his body, whereas anyone else who did not have this word would have sunk, should we really say, then, that there is no difference between our bodies and the body of Christ, since the word exists about Christ's body, "This is My body; this is My blood, etc."?

Second, this body alone, by the personal union, has been united to the divinity, which shines forth in that entire mass. **Third**, this body alone sits at the right hand of the power and majesty of God, above every name which is named, both in this age and in the one to come. Therefore, since Christ Himself expressly affirms the presence of His body in the Supper, and since it is agreed that His body has the most excellent prerogatives beyond our own bodies, what madness is it to deny and elude this, simply because it is not a property of our bodies?

Ambrose rightly says, "When Scripture expressly predicates and affirms something about the body of Christ, we should not seek the order of nature in that body, which was conceived supernaturally by the Holy Spirit and born of the virgin, etc."

But just because the human mind cannot comprehend how, according to the word, He can be in many different places at once, wherever the institution of the Supper is being observed, while keeping the truth of the human nature intact, that is certainly no reason to depart from the manifest words, for in this way the entire faith is overthrown. Hugh [of St. Victor]'s statement is quite elegant: "When you look at something and think to yourself, How can this be?, simply think about who is doing it, and it stops being an astonishing thing, or at least it will not be unbelievable. If the doer is thought to be omnipotent, then nothing will be impossible, etc."

Indeed, it is customary in Scripture that, when God reveals His will with a clear word, He leads faith to consider His omnipotence, like Abraham in Genesis 18 and Romans 4; Moses in Numbers 11; Mary in Luke 1; the Sadducees in Matthew 19; and in Philippians 3 with regard to the glorification of our bodies.

However, we do not separate God's power from His will. As Tertullian says, "God could have made man able to fly. But He did not make him this way simply because He could have. For it is written, 'He has done everything that He has willed.'" But since Christ, with express and clear words, revealed His will concerning the presence of His body and blood, both before and after His ascension, we combine His power with that revealed will, and we conclude with Abraham, "That which He has promised, He is also able to do." Therefore, it is clear that no true contradiction exists between the doctrine of the true human nature in Christ and concerning His presence in the Supper, according to the Word.

To this point pertain also the remaining arguments of this kind; the resolution and explanation of them are drawn from the same foundations. As the angel said, "He is not here; He has risen. He goes before you into Galilee, just as He said to you." In that case, the reason for the consequence is not, "He is in Galilee; therefore, He cannot be in Judea," for He immediately appears to Mary Magdalene near the tomb. But the "maxim" (as they call it) is, "just as He said to you." Indeed, we must truly admire the holy simplicity of the angel, since the nature and condition of the body of Christ was undoubtedly, in many ways, better known to him than to us. And yet when he goes to speak about Him, he directs himself back to the Word. "He said to you that He would not be in the tomb after the third day. Therefore, you should not seek the living among the dead." Let us also imitate this angelic simplicity. Let us not subject the body of Christ to our argumentations, either about ubiquity or about locality, but let us think, believe, and speak about Him "just as He said." The same One who said that His body would not be in the tomb after the third day also said with a solemn affirmation, "This is My body." Therefore, just as the angel rightly argued, "He is not here, just as He said to you," so we, too, rightly conclude from the same maxim, "He said, 'This is My body.' Therefore, He is truly present." For we have learned from the angel what we are to think about the body of Christ: "just as He said to us."

They also cite that passage from Philippians 3:

"He will conform the body of our humility to His own glorious body." Therefore, whatever our bodies cannot do, we should not believe that Christ's body can do, even though Scripture affirms it, etc.

But who is so impudent that he will dare to affirm that there will be no difference at all between the glorified bodies of the saints and that body which alone was made the property of the Word, and to which alone it was said, "Sit at my right hand"? Yet Paul says even of the saints, "As star differs from star in brilliance, so will be the resurrection of the dead, etc."

Nor should those who wish to be leaders of this battle use the following argument:

Christ says in Luke 24, "Touch and see, etc." Therefore, although Christ says, "This is My body," nevertheless, because He is not seen and touched, He is not truly and substantially present.

But what will be made of these arguments in the end? Will the definition of faith finally be sought, not from Hebrews 11, "of the things not seen," but from that Plautinian saying, "Our faith is a matter of sight; it believes what it sees"? When Stephen was in the Praetorium, he saw Jesus standing at the right hand of God. Therefore, was He not at the right hand of God before, when Stephen was not seeing Him? Indeed, while Stephen saw Him, the rest did not see Him. Likewise in Luke 24, when He disappeared and was rendered invisible, where was that saying then, "Touch and see"? Long ago the Holy Spirit was given through visible gifts. Shall we not believe, since we do not see, although we have the promise?

I recite these arguments, not because they require some eloquent refutation, but that we may consider what kind of foundation it is upon which those who depart from the clear words are demanding that our faith should be built.

Finally, to this point pertains that oft-cited Epistle of Augustine *Ad Dardanum*,[3] which practically always fills both the first and the last pages of their writings, because they say that, in

3 Augustine, Epistle 187

this Epistle, Augustine describes the common faith of the whole Church; namely, that the body of Christ must be in one certain place in heaven, after the manner of a genuine body, etc. But let us avoid lengthy discussions with a brief and simple response, which is, nonetheless, entirely certain. In truth, Augustine himself concludes that extended disputation in the same Epistle with these words: "If you find that anything in the work of our pen has been elaborated usefully, give thanks to God. If, however, you perceive any of my vices, then forgive as a dear friend does, namely, with the same sincerity of love, desiring for me the medicine whereby you also grant a pardon, etc."

Augustine does not tend to speak in this way when he is setting forth articles of faith; in that case, he tends to thunder with a powerful assertion: "This is what we say, what we strive to prove in many ways, etc." Likewise, in each article of faith in *De fide ad Petrum,* he repeats that preface, "Hold steadfast and in no wise doubt, etc."

Therefore, since he does not set forth this opinion (that the body of Christ must remain in one place in heaven) as an article of faith whose sure and immovable foundations he considers from the Word of God, but is merely expounding his own thoughts, for which he also begs to be forgiven if there is anything wrong with them, we would surely do foolishly if we were to depart from the sure and clear words of Christ on account of the personal thoughts of Augustine, in which he himself hardly confides, nor dares to affirm that they are true or certain.

We are seeking firm and solid arguments in this whole matter, not the kind of conjectures of whose uncertainty the authors themselves openly speak. Indeed, it can be understood from that final clause what we should rightly and truly judge concerning that whole disputation of Augustine. In the second book of Maccabees, there is a passage about prayers for the dead. But since the author concludes that book as he does ("If well, this is also what I myself have desired. But if less worthily, I must be pardoned"), we are not willing to be held by his authority, but we grant him the forgiveness for which he himself asks. For the canonical books do not speak in this way, but rather, "Thus says the Lord." "We know that his testimony is true, etc." And yet, 2 Maccabees is of greater value than Augustine's Epistle *Ad Dardanum*.

We will answer these things very simply, both to Augustine and to others among whom similar statements are read. We grant that, according to physical location, the body of Christ reclined at Supper and lay in the tomb. The Judge will return in the clouds in such a way that every eye will see Him. These things are very sure, since prior to any of that He was born of the Virgin Mary. Surely His flesh was not outside His mother's womb! But since Christ, who reclines at table and later resides in heaven, affirms with clear words that His body is present and distributed in the Supper, if the Zwinglians want us to depart from the sure sense of the clear words, then it must be proven by them that the power of Christ has been limited to such a degree that He cannot in another way, beyond that local, circumscribed, and visible manner, truly be present in the Supper with the substance of His body, as He said. Surely none of the ancient and approved writers, when they spoke about locality and circumscription, used that argument in such a way that he therefore took away and removed the substance and presence of the body and blood of Christ from the Lord's Supper. Indeed, this response rightly and truly stands against those many and lengthy citations.

These are, if not all, then surely the chief arguments which are usually presented from the article of the genuineness of the human nature in Christ.

XXIV. Arguments from the article of the ascension.

"Christ ascended into heaven with His body (Acts 1). He was received into heaven (Acts 3). He sits at the right hand of God the Father, etc. But the Lord's Supper is celebrated on earth. Therefore, the body and blood of Christ cannot truly and substantially be present there. For when Scripture wants to signify a very great distance, it speaks thus: Isaiah 55, 'As the heavens are exalted from the earth.' Psalm 102, 'According to the height of heaven from the earth, etc.'"

ANSWER

It is certain that "ascension" in this article does not only signify "disappearance," as Christ was made invisible in Emmaus, for the Evangelists describe the ascension thus in Acts 1: "He was lifted up, and a cloud received Him from their eyes. And while they were looking into heaven as He was going." Luke 24: "He withdrew from them and was taken into heaven." Likewise, "He will come from heaven in the clouds." Therefore, the words remain in their simple and proper meaning: Before the Last Judgment, Christ will not go about on this earth in the same manner and in the same way as He walked on the earth prior to His ascension, in a visible and physical location and circumscription of His body. For Scripture says, "He will come in the same way as you saw Him go into heaven." But this is the question: Does Christ's ascension into heaven comprise nothing greater or loftier than a change in location, as when little birds leave the ground and settle on top of a tree? Elijah was taken up into heaven in a whirlwind, and Elisha rightly says about that ascension, "There is no reason you should seek him on the earth, neither in the mountains nor in the valleys, for he has been taken up into heaven." Now, if there is no difference at all between the ascension of Christ and the assumption of Elijah, then the reasoning will be entirely the same and the logical consequence of the Zwinglians will be valid. For this is how they twist the statement of Peter in Acts 3: They interpret it in such a way that Christ must be firmly held by heaven, since Peter says that Christ must receive heaven. In German, this is expressed better, "*den Himel einnemen* – must take up heaven." But as with all of Holy Scripture, so also the article of the ascension is not of private interpretation, but the genuine and true sense of it must be sought from the explanation of the Holy Spirit Himself.

Peter, therefore, in Acts 2, interprets that article ("He ascended into heaven") according to the passage from the Psalm, "Sit at My right hand." For he says, "David did not ascend into heaven, and yet he says, 'The Lord said to my Lord, "Sit at My right hand."'" And Peter immediately explains what it means to sit at God's right hand when he says, "The right hand of God is exalted." Likewise, "God made Him both Lord and Christ." So, too, Christ Himself says in Luke 22, "The Son of Man will be sitting at the right hand of the power of God." And in Ephesians 4, Paul expressly sets out to explain that question for himself: "What does it mean that He ascended, except that He first descended into the lower regions of the earth? But He who descended is that same One who ascended above all the heavens, that He might fill all things. And He gave some, etc." Likewise, "He ascended on high; He led captivity captive; He gave gifts to men, etc."

Therefore, the article of Christ's ascension entails the highest exaltation and loftiness; it is a description of Christ as He gloriously reigns, that He who was crucified in weakness now lives in the power of God (2 Cor. 13).

Therefore, it is clear that there is an infinite difference between the ascension of Christ and the assumption of Elijah: not only that Christ ascended by His own power, but that, by the ascension, the Father lifted Him up to the highest place and placed Him at the right hand of the power of God, also according to His human nature. It is great madness, says Cyril, to understand by the session at God's right hand some sort of place, as perhaps the mother of Zebedee's sons understood, or like the thief hanging at Christ's right hand. For Scripture calls it "the right hand of the majesty" (Heb. 1), and of "the power of God" (Luke 22); "exalted to the right hand of God" (Acts 2). And it expressly explains what it means to sit at God's right hand in 1 Pet. 3: "Who is at the right hand of God, having gone into heaven, with angels and authorities and powers subject to Him." Eph. 1, "Seating Him at His right hand in the heavenly places, above every principality, authority, dominion, and every name which is named, not only in this age, but also in the one to come, and has placed all things under His feet, etc." Therefore, we have it from the certain and clear declaration of the Holy Spirit what the article of Christ's ascension into heaven entails.

Now it will be easy to discern, when Christ says, "This which is present, offered, and received in the Supper is My body and My blood," whether the article of the ascension itself prevents Him from being able to be truly and substantially present on account of the fact that there is a very great distance between heaven and earth. For, **first**, before He received heaven, He said at that first Supper, "This is My body, etc." And at that time there could certainly be no contradiction from the article of the ascension. He said, moreover, "Do this; namely, what I Myself have done at the first Supper." **Second**, after the ascension, while He was already residing on high, He delivered to Paul that the bread which is broken on earth in the Lord's Supper is His body, and that the cup which we bless in this world below is His blood. Therefore, that apparent contradiction from the article of the ascension was refuted by Christ Himself, for after He was received into heaven, He commanded Paul to pass on to the churches, "That which you take and eat on earth in the Eucharist is My body." **Third**, let us present the argument in those words with which the article of the ascension is described in Scripture. Christ ascended into heaven in such a way that, also according to His human nature, He was exalted to the highest place, above all creatures, to the right hand of the power of God, so that He says, "All authority in heaven and on earth has been given to Me, etc." And let us now consider whether this follows logically: Although He says, "This is My body," nevertheless, since the distance between heaven and earth is immense, He cannot be present in the Supper. Surely no sane person will claim that this is truly logical! No, Christ said, "This is My body," and at His ascension He sat down at the right hand of the power of God, also according to His human nature, so that all power is given to Him, etc. Therefore, He is powerful to do what He has said, since He did not ascend as Elijah did.

And lest anyone should imagine with great absurdity from the article of the ascension such an inclusion of Christ's body in heaven that He can only be in one place, even though He affirms with a clear word that it is His body which is present and offered, wherever the institution of the Supper is observed, Paul expressly meant to speak as he did in Ephesians 4: "He ascended above all the heavens, that He might fill all things." In Hebrews 5: "We have a High Priest who has entered heaven." Hebrews 7: "He was made higher than the heavens." So it is that the article of the ascension neither denies nor removes the true and substantial presence of Christ's body in the Eucharist. But since Christ promised with a clear word that His body would be present there, the article of the ascension confirms that Christ can do this with His body, since He sat down at the right hand of the power of God, although we do not comprehend how it is done.

XXV. The argument from the statements of Christ's going over from this world.

"John 16: 'I leave the world and go to the Father.' But clearly the Supper is celebrated in this world. Therefore, just as Christ left the world with the presence of His body and blood, so also He left His Supper which He instituted to be celebrated in this world."

"Matthew 26: 'The poor you have with you always, but Me you do not always have.' This cannot be understood concerning the divine nature which fills all things. Therefore, it must be understood concerning the body of Christ. If it cannot be had, then neither is it truly and substantially offered and received in the Supper."

ANSWER

In the articles of faith, whenever some apparent contradiction is suggested, we should not be immediately moved to another understanding than that which has been revealed in the words. For Paul delivers that final precept to Timothy, "Guard the deposit, avoiding the contradictions of what is falsely called knowledge; by professing it some have wandered away from the faith." [2 Tim. 1] It is not a new occurrence, then, that clever men are able to think up various contradictions against all the articles of faith. But Paul says, "If you want to guard the deposit, avoid those contradictions." Indeed, there is a truly glorious example in the story of Abraham, which I will note here before I proceed to the solution. God had commanded Abraham, "Take your son and sacrifice him as a burnt offering." [Gen. 22] In those words, there is neither obscurity nor ambiguity *per se*. But if Abraham had wanted to indulge his own thoughts, he could have easily—and indeed, seemingly plausibly—found a contradiction. For, **first**, the negative is expressly stated in Scripture in Genesis 9: "Whoever sheds human blood, etc." **Second**, that command is diametrically opposed, not only to the common teaching of Scripture, but also to that loftiest and greatest promise, "In Isaac shall your seed be called." [Gen. 21] O immortal God! If the Sacramentarians could produce contradictions like these, what victory parades would they prepare! But see how attentively Abraham's faith observes that Pauline commandment: "Avoid the contradictions of that which is falsely called knowledge." For undoubtedly his fatherly heart was stricken with various thoughts. Nor was he so unskilled in the Chaldean arts that he could not find some figure of speech which would enable him both to hold onto his only son whom he loved, but also to seem to satisfy God's command. But since he had an express mandate, given with certain, proper, and clear words, and since God did not reveal to him with His Word that it was to be interpreted as a metaphor, therefore, although it seemed to be at odds with the promise about Isaac, he did not fabricate figures of speech in order to elude the simplicity of God's command. But the Epistle to the Hebrews says that he reasoned thus: "Since both things are the Word of God, who cannot lie—both, 'Sacrifice your son!' and 'In Isaac shall your seed be called!'—therefore, the one thing I must do, and yet the other thing I must believe." [Heb. 11] And with regard to those two things which seemed to be at odds with one another, Abraham reasoned: "I believe that God, who said both things, is able to cause them not to be at odds with one another. For He is even able to raise my son from the dead, so that, in this way, both things are true, because both things are the Word of God."

I have recited these things at the beginning so that we do not allow our faith, which depends on certain and firm foundations of Scripture, to be disturbed with objections which have some appearance of a contradiction.

Therefore, let us consider whether in these sentences about the going over of Christ from this world, the negative ("It is not My body") has been expressed more clearly than the affirmative in the words of institution ("This is My body"). For that is necessary above all, if we are supposed to depart from the clear words.

First, this is clear: When, in the first Supper, Christ said to His disciples, "Take, eat. This is My body, etc.," He had not yet at that time left the world, and therefore the saying which was afterward both spoken and fulfilled (namely, "I leave the world, etc.") could not conflict with those words, "This is My body, etc.," in the first Supper. Furthermore, it is most certain from the Word of God that the same thing is given to us, and that we receive the same thing which the disciples received in the first Supper from the hands of Christ Himself. Therefore, those sentences do not provide us with a sufficiently certain and firm reason to depart from the clear words with which Christ affirms, "This is My body."

Second, this, too, is clear, that those two things are connected to one another and correspond mutually with one another: "I went out from the Father and came into the world. Again I leave the world and go to the Father," and that the true explanation of one member depends on the sense of the corresponding part. Now, it is not said only about the human nature of Christ, "I went out from the Father," since His sending should not be ascribed only to the one nature. Nor does it signify some local change, as if Christ left that place where the Father is, since it was written about Him, "I fill heaven and earth." But He is speaking about that mission on which He was sent from the Father, that He might become the Apostle and High Priest of our confession, that is, the victim for the sins of the whole world. This is why Christ's going over to the Father is our righteousness, not on account of a change of location. Nor can this be denied: That John, in his Gospel narrative, speaks differently about the world than Aristotle defines it to Alexander, as a system of heavenly and earthly bodies. Therefore, "to come into the world" means that the Son of God assumed the human nature, and not this only, but that the world also hated Him, persecuted Him, and finally nailed Him to a cross, and that He was tempted with all human infirmities, according to human likeness, without sin. And, on the other hand, "to leave the world" means (as the adversaries themselves interpret it) no longer to be exposed to the hatred, persecution, and injustices of the world, that is, of the devil and of the wicked; and, having set aside the infirmities, to enter into that glory which He had with the Father before the world was made, etc. When these things are considered in this way, what assurance can our conscience possibly have that it should depart from the clear and manifest words ("This is My body") on account of those statements, "I leave the world and go to the Father"? For also in John 8, when He said, "I am going, and where I go, you cannot come," the Jews did not understand it concerning a long-lasting departure or about a special interval, but they said, "Surely He is now going to kill Himself, since He said, 'Where I go, you are not able to follow.'" [John 8] It is the same as if someone argued thus: Since Christ was sent to become a victim for the sins of the world, He took up our infirmities, being exposed to the injustices and troubles of this world. But now, having set aside the infirmities, He reigns from the power of God, for this is what it means to leave the world (John 16). Therefore, although He manifestly affirms, "This is My body," He cannot be present. And the reason is that now He has entered into His glory. Yes, what a beautiful conclusion!

Third, no one can give a surer explanation of those statements ("I leave the world"; "You do not always have Me") than He who made them. Therefore, if we can produce the interpretation of Christ Himself as to how He left the world and how we do not always have Him, then surely all disputes should be settled, for it is written, "Hear Him!" Likewise, "Let all flesh keep silent before Him."

Therefore, in Luke 24, after Christ rose from the dead, He stood in the midst of His disciples and said, "These are the words which I spoke to you while I was still with you." You hear clearly that what He had said in John 15 was fulfilled at that time, "I leave the world." Or in Matthew 26, "You do not always have Me." Now, if you ask, "How did Christ leave the world? How do the disciples not always have Him?," the Sacramentarians respond that it must be understood concerning the body, flesh, and human nature of Christ. But Christ's explanation clearly refutes this interpretation when He affirms that He had already then left the world, and that He was already at that time no longer with the Apostles, even when He shows Himself to be present with His body, so that He says, "Touch and see!" And He showed them His hands and His feet, etc. Nor was this explanation invented recently, for Augustine says in Tractate 64 on John that the interpretation of that saying, "I am with you a little while longer," and of similar sayings, must be drawn from that passage, "These things I said to you while I was still with you."

Therefore, whoever denies the presence of Christ's body in the Eucharist on account of those sayings ("I leave the world." "You do not always have Me.") surely uses, not only sand, but hay and stubble for a foundation!

Finally. Since Christ Himself says that He is not with His disciples, that is, that He has left the world, and that the saying has been fulfilled, "Me you do not always have," at that very time when He shows Himself to His disciples as being present according to His body, flesh, and human nature, we correctly interpret those sayings concerning the weak, passible, mortal, and familiar custom of Christ, as He had previously walked with His disciples, as the text itself quite clearly shows. For we read this in Mark: "The poor you have with you always, and you can do good to them whenever you wish. But Me you do not always have, namely, so that you can do good to My body as to the poor whenever you want, with external kindnesses, as Mary now does when she anoints Me, etc." [Mark 14] And after the resurrection, Matthew writes that the women embraced Christ's feet when they first saw Him, and that He was not reluctant to allow this, in order that He might prove the truth of the resurrection. But when Magdalene clung to Him in a similar way and remained there as if she would hold onto Christ in that familiar custom and intimacy as before, He said to her, "Do not touch Me, but say to My disciples, 'I am ascending to My Father and your Father, etc.'" Thus also Jerome explains in commenting on Matthew 26, "Another question arises: Why did the Lord say to His disciples after His resurrection, 'I am with you till the end of the age,' whereas He now says to them, 'Me you do not always have'? But it seems to me that, in this passage, He is speaking about His bodily presence, that He will not be with them after the resurrection as He now is, with full intimacy and familiarity." These are Jerome's words. Augustine says the same thing in Tractate 64 on John when explaining those sayings, "I am with you a little while longer, etc.," and, "While I was still with you, etc." He distinguishes the presence of Christ in this way: First, He was present in mortal weakness, in which He walked with His disciples up until His Passion. Second, with a bodily, visible, palpable presence, as He walked with His disciples during the 40 days until His Ascension. He says that the third mode of presence is that with which He is with His own till the end of the age. And from this it is rightly understood how it is that Augustine sometimes denies and sometimes affirms the corporal presence of the body of Christ. Indeed, many statements of the ancients can be settled based on this understanding.

Chrysostom, too, when discussing the body and blood of the Lord in the Eucharist in Homily 60 to the people of Antioch, brought up the objection concerning that passage, "Me you do not always have, etc." Now, without a doubt, if the Church of that age had imagined the absence of the body of Christ in the same way as the Sacramentarians now teach, even if he had spoken "hyperbolically" (as the Sacramentarians falsely claim) about the presence of the body of Christ in his preceding statements, then on the occasion of that objection, he would surely have issued at least one word of instruction about the absence of the substance of the body of Christ when he expressly dealt with that matter, namely, what we receive and eat in the Eucharist. But he merely contrasts it with the passage, "I am with you always, to the end of the age." He likewise says, "When Elijah was taken up in the fiery chariot, he left his cloak behind for his disciple, Elisha. But when Christ ascended into heaven, He took His flesh with Him, and at the same time He left behind His flesh." Thus far Chrysostom. Nor can this statement of Chrysostom be understood concerning our flesh which is of the same substance as the flesh of Christ, for he is speaking there about the Eucharist. And a little earlier he said those words, "After Christ ascended into heaven, He left His flesh behind for us wrapped up in the mystery of the Sacrament."

Therefore, we have shown that those sayings about leaving the world and going over to the Father, etc., do not provide any sufficiently certain or firm reasons to depart from the proper and native sense of those words, "This is My body."

XXVI. Arguments from the passages about spiritual eating.

These are their words:

> It is certain that the sum and goal of that which Christ intended in the institution of the Supper is this: That His body, insofar as it was given for us, should become ours; that His blood, which was shed for the remission of sins, should be applied to us, together with all the things which He obtained and merited by the giving of His body and the shedding of His blood, etc. But we can gain all this from spiritual eating, even if the body and blood of the Lord are not truly and substantially present, given, and received. Therefore, although the presence of the substance of the body and blood of Christ has been removed from the Eucharist, we have, nonetheless, a splendid meal. Indeed, it is the more splendid, because we come to it through better instruments and by more excellent means, namely, with the mind and the intellect.

ANSWER

By the same rationale, there is no need to employ the elements of bread and wine. For even outside the use of the Supper, when faith strengthens itself in the strife so that a person determines with certainty that the body of Christ was given for him, etc., then we spiritually eat the flesh of Christ, etc. Why, then, should we not abandon the entire action of the Supper as useless? If they answer, "Because Christ commanded us to employ the elements of bread and wine," then we, too, have an answer: The same Christ, in the same institution, said, "This which you receive and eat is My body, etc." Indeed, it is obvious that there is more weight in these words of Christ than there is in the words, "Take bread, etc." For Paul does not say, "He will be guilty of the bread and the wine," but, "of the body and blood of the Lord."

For it is sure and certain that a twofold eating of the body of Christ is described in the words of the Supper. The first is sacramental, in these words, "Take, eat. This is My body. Drink. This is My blood, etc." For if these words were merely commandments to be fulfilled spiritually by the soul, there would be no need to take anything by means of the body or the mouth in the Supper. But this is false, for He does not say, "Take, eat bread." He says, "That which you thus take and eat with the mouth is My body." Likewise, if those words were merely to be understood of a spiritual eating, then no one could eat judgment on himself. No one could drink unworthily, contrary to the clear words of Paul. It is entirely certain, therefore, that the body of Christ is to be eaten in the Supper, not only spiritually, but also sacramentally, in the way previously described. But to the spiritual eating pertain those words, "Given and shed for you for the remission of sins. This do in remembrance of Me, etc."

Therefore, we teach, according to the words of Christ, both forms of eating in the Supper. And we expressly affirm that the sacramental eating without the spiritual eating is not only not beneficial, but, as Paul says, "He eats judgment on himself, etc." "He will be guilty of the Lord's body, etc.," if indeed we satisfy (as Cyprian says) the institution when we hear and do what Christ Himself, the Giver and Author of this Sacrament, did and commanded to be done.

The response to the arguments of the Zwinglians about spiritual eating is very obvious. Merely consider how much temerity (lest I speak more harshly) is involved when the Son of God invites us poor wretches to His table and says, "I want to join Myself to you, not only spiritually, but also in this most intimate manner. What you receive with the mouth is My body, is My blood." And then someone responds, "Lord, there is no need. That eating does us no good, for we are able to ascend into heaven by faith, and there apprehend You in Your majesty, and thus we are able to have a purer Supper." Consider, I say, what horrendous impiety this is, given that this meal is so important to Christ, who has invited us to it, though we are most unworthy.

Therefore, we should not say, "We can accomplish the eating of the body of Christ in a more suitable way or with more excellent instruments than with the mouth and the body." For Christ was made for us wisdom from God, and since He instituted a twofold eating of His body, it is clear what we are to do. So let us give thanks with all our heart to our Samaritan, to whom the weakness, corruption, and evil of our wounded and despoiled nature was not unknown, and yet He instituted not only one means, but several means for arousing, nourishing, and strengthening our faith. Nor should that ancient serpent suggest to us, "What need is there? You already have what you seek," or, "You can obtain the same thing in another way." But let us attribute this much wisdom to Christ our Lord, who was made for us wisdom from God, that the miserable condition of our nature was better known to Him than it is to us. And so let us, with the godly and reverent gratitude of our hearts, use those things which He instituted for the strengthening of our faith, which is not only assailed by weakness, but is also nearly overwhelmed by the corrupt wickedness of the flesh. If we were angels, as Chrysostom says, the bare promise alone would suffice. But now in this great corruption, even with the support Christ affords in the Sacraments, the faith of many not only teeters and totters, but is entirely extinguished. Therefore, since He did not only want to join Himself to us spiritually, but also wanted to unite Himself to us in this venerable Sacrament through the substance of His flesh (as Hilary says), what else can or should the obedience of our faith do but acknowledge and celebrate the immense love of God's Son toward us? Indeed, what surer pledge of our salvation could there be? What more effective method of strengthening our faith against the temptations of Satan and the wickedness of the flesh? For He not only dwells in us by His Spirit, but also mingles Himself with us by His body and blood, as Chrysostom says, in such a way that He changes us into Himself, so that we no longer remain flesh of Adam's flesh, but are made into members of His body, of His flesh and of His bones, as we explained more fully in the beginning.

XXVII. Arguments from John chapter six.

This argument seems very attractive:

> Christ speaks in the Supper about giving His body and shedding His blood, and He speaks of the same things in John 6. Similarly, He says that His body is to be eaten and His blood drunk in the Supper, and He also says the same thing in John 6. Therefore, it is certain that the body of Christ must be eaten and His blood drunk. But if one asks what the manner or mode of eating is, surely it cannot be better or more definitively explained than it is in John 6, for there the spiritual eating of the body of Christ is described at length.

ANSWER

We showed earlier that, in the words of institution, Christ did not only give the command about eating His body and drinking His blood, but He also described a twofold manner of eating; namely, a sacramental and a spiritual. Therefore, if the question is, in what way is the body of Christ, which is truly and substantially present and given in the Supper, to be taken so that a person does not eat judgment on himself and become guilty of the body of Christ, but is able to receive it for salvation, this is the right response: It should be taken with the same faith with which Christ also wants His body to be eaten outside the use of the Supper, John 6. And, in this way, the ancients not unsuitably accommodated the doctrine which is presented in John 6 to the Lord's Supper. But if one asks about the sacramental eating of the body of Christ, it is clear and certain that this eating is not described in John 6. For in the Last Supper, Christ first instituted that new and special manner. "This which you take and eat with the mouth is My body." In no way, therefore, is the following argument logical: In John 6, a merely spiritual eating of the body of Christ is described. Therefore, a merely spiritual eating is also described in the Supper. For in the institution, Christ did not merely institute the eating, but also a new and peculiar manner of eating which had not formerly existed in the Church. Therefore, that eating should not be learned from John 6, but from the words of institution. Indeed, it is useful to consider what the difference is between John 6 and the institution of the Supper, for in this way the matter will be clearer in the face of all kinds of sophistry.

First. The sermon in John 6 took place more than a year before the institution of the Supper, for Paul says about the Supper, "On the night in which He was betrayed, etc." But John numbers three Passovers, and before the second Passover he says that the events occurred which are described in John 6. Therefore, it is a false claim made by some that John 6 describes the institution of the Supper.

Second. The Capernaites in John 6 were looking for a supper made up of external bread, as Christ says, "You seek Me because you ate of the loaves of bread and were filled." But He says, "I am not speaking to you about eating external bread. No, you must eat My flesh!" In the Supper, however, the elements of bread and wine are required, for He took the bread and said, "Eat. This is My body." He took the cup and said, "Drink. This is My blood." And He adds, "This do." Therefore, if someone were to contend that the elements of bread and wine in the Supper should be abandoned, since they are not only not employed but are expressly rejected in the eating of John 6, he would surely go shamefully astray. It is clear, therefore, that the sixth chapter of John does not remove those things which were expressly instituted in the Supper.

Third. The bread, the cup, the eating, and the drinking in John 6 are, without any controversy, taken figuratively. For in that text the figure of speech is expressly explained. But in the Supper, it is clear that those things are properly understood without a figure of speech. For when Christ says to His disciples, "Take, eat, and drink, etc.," surely He means that they should take it with the mouth, which is not required in John 6.

Fourth. Since the eating in John 6 entails the application of the benefits of the body and blood of Christ through faith, it is always used by everyone for eternal life. But in the Supper, many eat the body of the Lord for the judgment of eternal damnation and become guilty of Christ's body.

Fifth. The eating in John 6 is and should be done at all times and in all places. But it is written of the sacramental eating, "as often as you drink it," and, "when you come together."

This is a clear difference between the eating of John 6 and the eating which was instituted in the Supper, and from this difference many clouds of equivocations are dissipated. As Augustine says, *De Doctrina Christiana*, Bk. 3, ch. 16: "If something is said in the form of a precept which seems to command a shameful act or a crime, then it is a figurative statement, such as, 'Unless you eat the flesh of the Son of Man and drink His blood, etc.' He seems to command a crime or a shameful act. Therefore, it is a figure of speech, prescribing that men must share in the Lord's suffering and that they must hold sweetly and effectively in their memory the fact that His flesh has been crucified and wounded for us." Likewise, what Origen says in Sermon 7 on Leviticus, chapter 10, treating those words, "Unless you eat the flesh, etc." He says: "Recognize that these are figures of speech, written in divine books." So also Chrysostom, Homily 46 on John, says: "Therefore, the Capernaites erred, for they understood the eating of John 6 simply, as the words sound, etc." The Zwinglians loudly repeat these things in order to remove the presence of Christ's body from the Supper by their own figure of speech. But it is crystal clear that the Fathers are speaking about the eating of John 6, which Christ Himself expressly shows in John 6 to be a figure of speech. But we have demonstrated that the eating which was instituted in the Supper is something else. If they want that eating to be figurative like the eating in John 6, then the Lord's Supper can be celebrated without bread and wine, and in such a way that the mouth receives nothing—which is clearly false. Therefore, it is a fallacy of equivocation. Indeed, Augustine rightly labels it a shame, a crime, and an outrage—that Scythian butchering of the body of Christ and the Cyclopian gulping of His gore, such as the Capernaites at one time imagined. But we stated above how the sacramental eating of the body of Christ is to be understood according to the words of institution. Therefore, since we have nothing in common with the Capernaites, Augustine's statement has nothing against us.

XXVIII. The argument from the words of institution, "This do in remembrance of Me." Likewise, "You will announce the death of the Lord until He comes."

In order that they may not seem to pass over the institution entirely, drawing no support from it at all, they snatch up those words, "This do in remembrance of Me."

"'This do in remembrance of Me.' But memory has to do with things that are either past or absent. Therefore, one should not believe in the true presence of the body and blood of Christ in the Supper."

ANSWER

First, let us consider here how trivial and frivolous is this foundation on which they command us to build our faith in such a lofty matter. Are we to conclude, then, that, for as long as the Apostles had Christ visibly present with them, they never remembered Him? Indeed, if remembrance requires and necessarily includes the absence of the one who is being remembered, then how could they have done the eating and drinking in remembrance of Him at that time when Christ was visibly present at the first Supper? For He did not only say, "This do in remembrance of Me," with regard to future Suppers. Even Oecolampadius himself recognizes the weakness of this argument, for he says, "Memory is often of things that are present. As the poet says, 'The Ithacan did not forget himself at such a crisis.'"

Furthermore, Paul uses that phrase, ἀναμιμνήσκω σε, "I remind you to stir up, etc.," in 2 Timothy 1, where he clearly does not refer to something absent, for he adds soon after, "the gift which is in you." But since he realized how easily that gift could be suffocated and extinguished, he proposed to Timothy a remembrance. Thus Christ has regard for the miserable corruption of our nature, which causes the memory of Christ and His benefits to be quickly erased from our minds and almost entirely buried. In order to renew, retain, and strengthen that memory, He says that He is instituting a very present remedy: the communion of His body and blood.

And if they want to make this a remembrance of something that is entirely past or absent, the answer is clear. For Paul explains that remembrance in this way: "You will announce the Lord's death, etc." So you have a past thing of which Paul prescribes a remembrance. He does not thereby remove the presence of the body of Christ, which is affirmed with clear words.

They also fabricate an argument from Paul's words in this way: "You will announce the Lord's death until He comes. Therefore, He is not present."

Likewise, from the article of faith, "From thence He will come, etc." Scripture only knows of two advents of Christ in the flesh, and He says that the second coming will not happen before the Last Day, describing it in this way: "As lightning flashes from the east to the west, so will be the coming of the Son of Man." Based on this, Zwingli says:

> If I saw the body of Christ descend like lightning into the bread, then I would be willing to believe its presence. For this is what the second coming of Christ will be like according to Matthew 24.

ANSWER

We believe and confess that the second coming of the Son of Man will not happen before the Last Day, and that it will not be hidden, but will be so glorious and evident that it will be known to the whole world. But in the Supper, we do not call it either a "descent" or a "coming" of the body of Christ into the bread, as we explained at the beginning from the words of Luther. But since the Son of God says, "This which you take is My body," we simply believe this and commend to divine omnipotence the manner in which it is present. For there is a difference here. Before His suffering, He was present in a weak and mortal way; after His resurrection, for 40 days until His ascension, He was present with a visible and palpable presence when He wished to be; on the Last Day, He will come in the clouds of heaven, with power and great glory. And then they will see the Son of Man coming. But meanwhile, up to the end of the age, until He comes in that visible majesty and glory, He says, "This which you take is My body and My blood." For one cannot apply to God the logical consequence: "He will come; therefore,

He is not present." Therefore, the two statements are by no means at odds with one another: "Until He comes," or, "from thence He will come," and, "This is My body." For Scripture calls that second and glorious coming of the Son of Man for judgment an "appearance" and a "revelation," ἐπιφάνειαν & ἀποκάλυψιν. 2 The. 2: "He will destroy him by the appearance of His coming." 1 Tim. 6: "Until the coming of our Lord Jesus Christ, which He will manifest (δείξει) in His own time, the blessed and only powerful, etc." 2 Tim. 4: "To all who love His appearance." Titus 2: "Awaiting the appearance of the glory of the great God." 1 Cor. 1: "Awaiting the revelation of our Lord Jesus Christ." 2 The. 1: "When the Lord Jesus is revealed from heaven, with the angels of His might, etc." But in the Lord's Supper, there is no descent, nor coming, nor appearance of the body and blood of Christ. For these things pertain to the second coming of the Son of Man on the Last Day. But we simply believe, according to the words of Christ, that His body and blood are truly present with the bread and wine in the Supper and are truly offered to those who eat and drink. For even before that appearance and revelation occur on the Last Day, Christ says, "Behold, I am with you until the end of the age." Likewise, "I will be in their midst." It is clear, therefore, that the sayings about the second coming of the Son of Man do not remove His true presence with which He has promised to be present for His Church, according to His own Word, until the end of the age, until He comes in the clouds of heaven, etc.

XXIX. The argument from the similarity of the Old Testament Sacraments.

"Concerning the Sacraments, a judgment must be made on the basis of similarity. But in the Old Testament, the name of something that is signified is often attributed to a sign, by metonymy. Therefore, just as the lamb was called 'the Passover,' and yet it was not substantially that passing-over angel, but was merely a sign and memorial of that passing over which had already occurred in the past—as the text says, 'The blood will be a sign to you, etc.,' likewise, 'You will keep this day as a memorial'—so also the bread is said to be the body of Christ, not because it is truly and substantially present, given, and taken with the bread, but because it is a sign and memorial of the body which was given and of the blood which was shed. Likewise, just as the cow in Numbers 19 is called 'sin,' and yet it is not really sin itself, but a sacrifice for sin, so those words, 'This is My body,' can be understood and explained either with regard to the signification or with regard to the power and efficacy of the absent body, or in another way."

ANSWER

There is undoubtedly some similarity among the Sacraments. But to judge from the similarity alone, by the past, proper, and peculiar institution of each Sacrament, and indeed, to extend the reckoning of the similarity to the point of affirming that something is to be believed contrary to the express words of institution, without a manifest declaration of the Holy Spirit, is clearly false. For this rule is true, perpetual, and immovable: One must judge concerning the Sacraments from the proper institution and description of each one, so that the reckoning of the similarity which exists among the Sacraments is to be drawn and governed, not from the doctrinal heading of similar things, but from the Word of God which deals peculiarly with each Sacrament. No one concluded anything about the Paschal lamb based on the institution of circumcision, but based on that Word of God with which that particular rite was first instituted.

As for the fact that the Passover is a sign and memorial of past deeds and a reminder of the coming deliverance, this is not determined from the doctrinal heading of similar things; there are clear testimonies in the Word of God in which its institution is treated (Exodus 12, and also 1 Corinthians 5, etc.).

Therefore, as much as they strive to lead this question away from the words of institution (for in this way they can arbitrarily invent and claim anything at all), so much should we diligently see to it that we always confine ourselves to the sources of the institution and keep all disputations within its boundaries and limits. For thus many deceptions will be exposed and all things will become clear. The following argument is one of those deceptions:

> The ancients had the same Sacraments as we do with regard to the essence and substance of the Sacraments. For in 1 Cor. 10, Paul says, "All ate the same bread and drank the same cup." But now, it is certain that, in the manna of the ancients, the body of Christ was not substantially present, for Christ had not yet been incarnated. Therefore, neither is it present in the Eucharist.

ANSWER

Let us first consider the serious cause that motivates the Zwinglians to proscribe the presence of Christ's body and blood from the Lord's Supper. The Son of God said, "This is My body." They, on the other hand, claim, "It is not." And they give as the reason that otherwise the Sacraments of the New Testament would have a certain prerogative ahead of the Sacraments of the ancients under the Law. This is also how Schwenckfeldt philosophizes:

> The presence of Christ's body and blood in the Eucharist cannot be proven from the Old Testament. Therefore, neither should it be believed according to the express word of the New Testament.

Even if nothing else is added, pious and sound minds should be content considering the nature of this argument. It was not said of the manna, "This is My body." Therefore, although Christ said of the bread which we break, "This is My body," it is not true. And the reason is that there should be no difference between the light of the New Testament and the shadows of the Old. But the rule is certain and immovable: One must determine the similarity or difference in the Sacraments from each one's institution.

But when they cite the passage in 1 Cor. 10, Paul simply tells us, as is clear from the text, that the ancients had the same food and drink in common with one another. "All our fathers ate the same food. But with most of them God was not well pleased." And thus also Oecolampadius explains it. He says, "A comparison should not be made with us, as some explain that they ate the same food as we do. But the comparison is made among themselves, so that the food which Moses ate was denied neither to Korah, nor to Abiram, nor to the women, etc." And yet we will not spend much time squabbling here, for the text itself brings with it the solution. It says, "They had the same spiritual food and the same spiritual drink." And again, the text itself explains what that spiritual food and drink is, saying, "The Rock, however, was Christ." Clearly the ancients had no other Christ than we in the New Testament have, for "Christ today, yesterday, and forever" (Heb. 13). Nevertheless, they did not have Him in the same way, for they believed in the One who was to come, while we believe in the One who was given, in the Word made flesh, who dwelt among us; who was found in condition as a man, etc. Jacob says, "I saw the Lord resting on a ladder which reached to the earth," which undoubtedly signified the future incarnation of Christ. But Jacob did not see in the same way as Thomas. The logical consequence would be: Jacob did not see the true flesh of Christ; therefore, it was also not the true and substantial flesh which the Apostles saw and handled. It must be a figure of speech!

Yes, if there should be no difference whatsoever between the shadows and the truth, then Christ must only be a man, for Melchizedek, who was a figure of Christ, surely was not God. Indeed, Christ must not be a rational man, for the lamb was a figure of Him. And in the end, life itself is hardly granted to Him, for the bronze serpent was a figure of Christ.

Likewise, if the food and drink is supposed to be entirely the same, then we should not be using bread in the Supper, but manna; not wine, but water from a rock. Now, if they try to make an exception here, claiming that there is a difference in the external symbols, since that difference is expressed with a clear word, we respond: That other difference is also expressed with words that are no less clear. For Christ says of the bread, "This is My body." This was not said of the manna. Why, then, do we not also observe that difference between the Sacraments of the Old and New Testaments, since it is much more important? For Paul says, "Whoever does not discern the Lord's body eats judgment on himself." Therefore, the whole dispute returns to this: We must judge what we are to understand and believe about the Lord's Supper, not from the similarities, but from the words of institution. Then the matter will be clear to those who piously seek the simple truth.

XXX. The argument from the statements of the ancients, who call the bread a sign or figure of the body of Christ.

Augustine, *De Trinitate*, Bk. 3, ch. 4, calls it "the Sacrament of the body of Christ." The same Augustine, *Contra Adimantum*, calls it "the sign of the body of Christ." And writing on Psalm 3, he calls it "the figure of the body and blood."

Jerome, commenting on Matthew 26: "He represented the truth of His body and blood with bread and wine."

Cyprian, Bk. 2, Epistle 3: "We see that the blood of Christ is revealed in the wine."

Ambrose, *De his qui initiantur mysteriis*: "After the consecration, the body of Christ is signified."

"Therefore, the dogma about the absence of Christ's body in the Eucharist was always received and approved from the beginning in the ancient and purer Church."

ANSWER

We clearly demonstrated above what the ancient Church concluded about the Lord's Supper, and these phrases—"the bread is a sign or figure of the body of Christ, etc."—are not at odds with that understanding. For the ancients, without transubstantiation, recognize two things in the Eucharist, as Irenaeus and Prosper say. First, the elements of bread and wine. Second, the body and blood of Christ. And sometimes they speak of both of those things together (as the Scripture itself does), while at other times they speak separately about only the one part. They speak often and very clearly about the presence of the body and blood of Christ. Indeed, they speak of it so splendidly, it is as if nothing remained there of the bread and wine. But sometimes they utter words about the elements and external signs themselves, which are subject to the senses. And just as the Papists do poorly when they force the fiction of transubstantiation on the Fathers based on the former passages, where they speak of the body of Christ without mentioning the element, so the Sacramentarians do no less poorly when they try to persuade the world, based on those passages where the Fathers speak about the external signs, as if antiquity denied the true presence of the body and blood of Christ in the Eucharist.

But even when the ancients call the bread a sign or a figure of the body of Christ, they affirm and confess its true presence so expressly and clearly that not even the adversaries can deny it. For Peter Martyr Vermigli teaches a certain rule with these words: "When one reads in the Fathers that the body of Christ is contained or held by these mysteries, nothing else is to be understood by those sayings than that it is indicated, revealed, demonstrated, and signified, etc." Therefore, it is clear even by the confession of the adversaries how the ancients understand the "sign and figure, etc."; namely, that the body of Christ is signified by the mysteries in such a way that it is contained and held by them. But let the honesty of their argument be weighed. The Fathers say both things, that the body of Christ is both signified and contained or held. The Sacramentarians, on the other hand, concealing and burying the second phrase, snatch up only the first and then bellow that the Fathers called it a "sign"! Likewise, they said that it was "signified." Therefore, it is not the communion of the present body!

Therefore, the terms "sign" or "figure" do not remove the true presence. For in the books about the Sacraments which are ascribed to Ambrose, the true presence of the Lord's body and blood in the Supper is asserted with a long discourse and with multiple arguments. In fact, it is asserted so clearly that even the Zwinglians reject those books. And yet in Book 4, chapter 5, it is called a "figure" of the body and blood of Christ.

But some of the ancients themselves expressly explain why they use those formulas, namely, that it is a sign or a figure.

Augustine, *De Catechisandis rudibus*, says: "They are visible signs of divine things, but the invisible things are honored in them."

He says the same thing, *De sententiis Prosperi*: "In the outward appearance of bread and wine, which we see, we honor the invisible things, that is, the flesh and blood of Christ, etc." For since, as said earlier, there are two things in the Eucharist, one of which can be neither seen there with the eyes nor comprehended with any sense. But the other has been exposed to the senses. They said that the visible element is a sign of the body—not the absent body, but the body that is truly, but invisibly, present, so that they declared that it is present there in a peculiar way, although not apparent to the eyes. And in the same mode of speaking, Augustine says about the cloud and flames that the Lord and Holy Spirit, who was invisible by nature, was revealed in those bodily forms. In that case, the absence promoted by the Zwinglians has no place.

So also Augustine calls it a "Sacrament" of Baptism, for "It is the water that is discerned, but the Spirit, who is not seen, is the one who works." In the same way, Chrysostom and Cyril call it a "Mystery" and "a mystic benediction," not on account of the absence of the body and blood of the Lord, but as Paul says of the Gospel, "We speak the wisdom of God in a mystery," and, "stewards of the mysteries of God, etc.," because that doctrine has been placed far above and beyond the sight of all reason. Moreover, it was revealed by the Son of God in the Word, and reason must be taken captive by faith for obedience to God. Thus, since the palate cannot make a judgment about the presence of the body and blood of the Lord in the Eucharist, the Fathers speak of a mystical food, because faith learns what it is and believes it to be true, not from the senses or from reason, but from the Word of God. Thus Hilary says, "He has added the nature of His flesh to the nature of eternity under the Sacrament in which He shares His flesh with us." Likewise, "We are in Him through the Sacrament in which He shares His flesh and blood."

This distinction is also helpful by way of explanation. When the ancients call the bread a sign, etc., they make an important distinction between the signs and figures which merely signified the absent and future body of Christ in the Old Testament. Cyril, for example, in his commentary on John, Bk. 4, ch. 28: "The setting of the table, then, that is, the showbread, most definitely signifies the most holy body of Christ with which all people are nourished for eternal life, etc." Surely it is not the same, is it, when David eats the showbread and when Paul says, "The bread which we break is a communion of the body of Christ"?

Tertullian says that wine was an ancient figure of the blood of Christ (Gen. 49, Isa. 63), since it merely signified it. But shall we say that, in the same way and for the same reason, the cup of blessing is the communion of the blood of Christ just as wine was drunk at the time of Isaiah, or when Lot became inebriated?

Chrysostom, commenting on John 6, after explaining many things about the drinking of the blood of Christ in the mysteries, adds this: "If its figure had so much power in the temple of the Hebrews, the smearing on the doorposts in the midst of Egypt, the truth has far more. This blood, in the figure, washed away sins, cleansed the Holy of Holies. If it had so much power in this figure, if death was so afraid of its shadow, how much more, I ask, will it shrink back in fear from the truth itself?" Yes, what clearer declaration could there be? For he expressly contrasts the figure of the blood of Christ in the Old Testament with the blood itself in the Eucharist.

We also have other statements of the ancients explaining why and in what sense they assign the terms "sign" or "figure" to the bread of the Lord's Supper. In his little work, Bessarion cites two statements, one of which is from Hilary: "The body of Christ in which we participate at the altar is a figure, insofar as the bread and wine are evident to the external senses. But it is the truth, insofar as the body and blood are believed in the truth of the heart." The second statement is by Augustine: "The body of Christ is both truth and figure. It is truth in as much as, by the power of the Holy Spirit, the body of Christ is produced from the substance of bread and wine. But that which lies before the external senses is a figure, etc."

The distinction is true, then: Some signs are merely significative, like Gideon's fleece. Other signs are exhibitive; they not only signify, but have and offer the very things of which they are signs. Thus the dove was a symbol of the Holy Spirit. In this way, the bread can be called a sign of the body of Christ.

But it is also helpful to observe that, in later times, various blasphemies against the truth have arisen from those terms, "sign, figure, etc." And, for this reason, those forms of speech have finally been repudiated and rejected as ambiguous and unhelpful, as is found, for example, in Damascenus, Bk. 4, ch. 14; in Theophylact on Matthew 26, Mark 14, John 6. I will also include here the words of Pomeranus, who writes in favor of the same opinion on Jonah: "It is perilous to speak of the 'Sacrament' of Baptism or the 'Sacrament' of the body and blood of the Lord. For Christ calls it, not a Sacrament or a sign, but a true Baptism in His Church, His true body and His true blood in His Supper. At the same time, however, I do not deny that they are signs which are performed externally in the ministry. But I want the truth itself, which is in the word of Christ's institution, to be wholly preserved for the Church also in the terms that are employed. For we have not yet forgotten that some in recent times have abused these words, 'the Sacrament of Christ's body,' as if the true body and the true blood of Christ were not given to us in the Supper, etc., but a sign of Christ's body and a sign of His blood, etc." Brenz says this: "It should be understood that the bread and wine of the Lord's Supper are not only bare signs of absent body and blood, but that they are truly Sacraments of the present body and blood, through which the body and blood of Christ are truly and presently offered and distributed to us." I consider these to be the chief arguments of the Zwinglians. For the arguments which are amassed in great number elsewhere can easily be brought under these headings. Indeed, I have wanted only to repeat the sources of the explanations which are presented more fully in the writings of others.

XXXI. Historical note: The struggles which have ensued in the Church concerning this controversy in every age up to our own times.

In all the articles of Christian doctrine, when an antithesis between a true and a false understanding is established, it is very useful to consider similar conflicts which have exercised the Church at various times; by which witnesses of the truth and by which arguments the budding errors were evaluated and refuted. I will not, however, set up a catalogue of all the corruptions and blasphemies of this holy mystery; this is not the place for it. But we will merely note briefly which erroneous opinions about this controversy—namely, opinions contrary to the true presence of the body and blood of the Lord in the Supper—were strewn about long ago, and how they were pressed back. And since there does not exist a sufficiently diligent record of these things in the ecclesiastical chronologies, it will have to be gathered from the writings of the ancients. But I will follow a chronological order.

I. **Theodoret** cites the epistle of Ignatius to the Smyrnans, in which he recounts, among the other writers of his time immediately after the Apostles, that certain heretics had arisen, denying that the Eucharist is the flesh of our Savior Jesus Christ. Among those epistles which are commonly ascribed to Ignatius, the seventh in the list is addressed to the Smyrnans, but mere trivialities are uttered there, namely, that only that Eucharist is authoritative and firm which is administered by the bishop. But Theodoret recounts these words of Ignatius concerning those heretics: "They do not admit the Eucharists and offerings, because they do not confess that the Eucharist is the flesh of our Savior Jesus Christ which suffered for our sins, which the Father raised up by His kindness, etc." Therefore, immediately after the times of the Apostles, disputes began to be stirred up concerning those words, "This is My body," so that the true presence of Christ's flesh was removed from the Supper.

II. **Justin** tells how the Gentiles wanted to imitate the rite of the Lord's Supper in such a way that, in the sacred rites of the sun, in the initiation of those who were first taking up the profession of that religion, they used bread and water, together with certain songs, as if the Lord's Supper in the Church were also merely a sign and token of the external profession. But Justin says, "We do not understand these things as common bread and normal drink.

But just as, through the Word of God, Jesus Christ our Savior was made Man and had both flesh and blood for our salvation, so also we have been taught that this food, which has been sanctified through the word given by Him, from which our flesh and blood are nourished κατὰ μεταβολήν - by a change, is the flesh and blood of the incarnate Jesus. For He said, 'This is My body; this is My blood.'" There is a parallel situation among the Jews, which their own treachery invented in order to mock the most holy mystery of the Lord's Supper. For among them, the head of the family picks up and sets aside a piece of the bread that has been placed on the table, gives thanks, breaks it, and distributes it to the family or guests.

III. **Irenaeus**, in Book 4, ch. 34, mentions that the heretics of his time who denied either the humanity or the divinity of Christ, or the article of creation, or the resurrection of the flesh, could not correctly understand that the Eucharist is made up of two things, an earthly and a heavenly. For he says, "They either change the sense or abstain from offering the things previously named. But our understanding of the Eucharist is harmonious, and the Eucharist, in turn, confirms our understanding."

And in Book 5, he says, "If Christ did not truly have flesh and blood, by which He has redeemed us, then neither is the cup of the Eucharist the communion of His blood, nor is the bread which we break the communion of His body. For the blood is none other than that which came from veins and flesh and the rest of the substance which is according to man, with which the Word of God was truly made. By His blood, He has redeemed us." And a little later, as he goes on to prove also that the flesh of believers is capable of eternal life, he says, "Not only the spiritual man, that is, the soul or the spirit, but also the flesh is fed and nourished by the body and blood of the Lord." He also says in Book 4, "Our bodies receive the Eucharist, which consists of two things." Indeed, he cites the passage from Paul: "Since we are members of His body, of His flesh and of His bones." He adds, moreover, "He is not talking about some spiritual and invisible man, for a spirit has neither bones nor flesh, but about that condition which is according to man, which consists in flesh and nerves and bones, which is nourished from the cup which is His blood, and which is edified from the bread which is His body."

IV. **Tertullian** says *In Apologetico*: "When the Gentiles heard that Christians eat the body and drink the blood of Christ in the Lord's Supper, they brought the Church into terrible disrepute, claiming that they butchered a baby at their meetings, sopped up its blood with bread, and thus consumed it. Indeed, even some of the heretics are said to have done something similar." But Tertullian merely responds: "There is no Scythian butchering of meat in the Supper, nor a Cyclopian gorging on human blood, as Catiline writes that his own conspirators bound themselves to one another by tasting the flesh and blood of a man they had slaughtered." He does not explain the true practice of the mysteries there, for it was sufficient to have refuted the crimes laid to their charge.

V. **Clement of Alexandria**, *Paedago.*, Bk. 2, ch. 2, gives this explanation of the words of the Supper: "'This is My blood,' namely the blood of the Vine, as Jacob says, 'He will wash His garment in the blood of grapes.' But what is added, 'which is shed for many for the remission of sins,' He says allegorically to signify the holy flow of happiness, namely, as wine gladdens the heart of man, so the preaching of the remission of sins is the joyful message of the Gospel." Surely this is an altogether profane opinion which is not found with any other ecclesiastical writer. And it is clear that Philosophy, which flourished at that time in the Alexandrian school, offended by this supernatural mystery of the presence and distribution of the body and blood of Christ, first began then to depart from the character of the words, in search of an allegorical interpretation (as the Alexandrian school was the workshop that produced the allegories to which not a few corruptions in doctrine are owed) which would allow for those things which seemed absurd to human reason in the Eucharist to be mitigated in such a way that the doctrine of the

Church might be rendered plausible also to the wise men of this age.

He says the same thing: "The blood of the Lord is twofold. The first is carnal, by which we are redeemed from ruin; but the second is spiritual, with which we are anointed. Indeed, this is what it means to drink the blood of Jesus, to be a partaker of the Lord's incorruptibility. And so, with the proportion and the consistency in the right measure, the wine is mixed with water, but the spirit is mixed with man. And the tempered wine he receives from the banquet for faith, while the spirit leads to incorruptibility. And the blending of both, namely, of the drink and of the word, is called the Eucharist. Those who are partakers of it by faith are sanctified in both body and soul, since the divine will has mystically brought man together by the Spirit and the Word, etc."

This opinion of Clement is new, therefore, and unknown to the more ancient writers. **First**, that Christ has a twofold blood, and that the words of the Supper do not speak of that true blood of Christ by which we were redeemed. But this is very clearly false. **Second**, that Christ is joined to believers only by the spirit, and that only the divinity of Christ makes believers alive, not His flesh. But this summary was often refuted by Cyril and was expressly condemned at the Council of Ephesus. **Third**, that the phrases, "to eat and to drink," in the words of the Supper, are to be taken metaphorically. But if this is true, then the institution of the Supper could be observed, even if the mouth received nothing, which everyone knows to be false. Likewise, the unworthy would not eat judgment on themselves, which is contrary to Paul. **Fourth**, Clement does shameful injustice to the words of institution by this explanation, "This is My blood, namely, the blood of grapes, which is called the blood of Christ as Creator and Lord." Origen drew many murky conclusions from the same pools of philosophy. For since he transformed all things into allegories, even the simplest and clearest statements, he played the same game also with the words of the

Supper. This, for example, is what he says on Matthew 26: "This bread which God the Word confesses to be His body, is the word which nourishes the soul, the word proceeding from God the Word. And this drink which God the Word confesses to be His blood is the word which splendidly gives drink and intoxicates the hearts of believers. This bread is the word of righteousness by which those who eat are nourished in their souls. But the drink is the word of the knowledge of Christ, according to the mystery of His nativity and passion." He says the same in Homily 9 on Leviticus: "Do not cling to the blood of the flesh, but learn the blood of the Word." And in Homily 7, he says: "As Christ speaks about the eating of His body, so also He says that Peter, Paul, the Apostles, and their disciples are the clean food for their neighbor." He clarifies how he wants this to be understood, saying, "When we sow the Word, it cannot be that we fail either to take or to furnish some flavor among ourselves, either from the response or from the question or from some gesture, etc." There is no need to add a refutation. Just consider how the simple words of institution—"This is My body which is given for you; this is My blood which is shed for you"—are mocked with these violent allegories. These, however, are not the only errors in Clement and Origen, with the result that Clement's writings are not undeservedly included by Gelasius among the apocryphal writings.

Chrysostom later expertly refuted that profane opinion, as if it were not the true and natural blood of Christ of which the words of the Supper speak. For example, in Homily 60 to the people of Antioch, after He mentioned the mouth and the tongue in the reception of the Eucharist, He said, "It is Christ's own blood which is received there." And in Homily 83 on Matthew he says, "Christ joins and binds Himself to us with His own body." Elsewhere He says that it is "the blood which flowed from Christ's side." He says the same in Homily 45 on John, and in Homily 60 and 61 to the people of Antioch, he repeats that statement, "Christ joins Himself to us, not only by faith and love, but in reality, through His body." And he says that this is done "through the food which He has given us, saying, 'Take and eat. This is My body, etc.'" It cannot be understood any better why Chrysostom emphasizes these things so often and with such precise words than by looking at the antithesis. For undoubtedly that philosophical opinion of Clement and Origen—that Christ joins Himself to believers only by spirit, that is, by divinity—clung to many disputes on account of the fame of the authors, even after their death, and therefore such a stern refutation needed to be repeated so often. But Cyril fights against that opinion even more splendidly, as a practical expert, as I will now explain.

VI. It is clear that, at the time of **Cyril**, the dispute had broken out again whose seeds had been previously sown by Clement; namely, that Christ dwells in believers only by His spirit, through faith and love, but that He is not joined to us by His flesh itself. Likewise, that our bodies do not depend on the flesh of Christ, as branches depend on a Vine, but only on His divinity. For with these words from Book 10, commenting on John 13, he expressly calls out a certain man by name and condemns and refutes that opinion with great vehemence and in many places, and he does it on the basis of the doctrine of the Lord's Supper. He says, "We do not deny that we are joined to Christ spiritually, by a right faith and by sincere love. But we emphatically deny that there is no way for us to be joined with Him according to the flesh, and we declare that such a notion is entirely foreign to the divine Scriptures. For who has doubted that Christ is also the Vine in this way, and we the branches who draw life for ourselves from Him, etc.? Likewise, is there anyone who thinks that we are ignorant of the power of the mystical benediction? Since this takes place within us, does it not also cause Christ to dwell in us bodily by the communion of His flesh?"

The Zwinglians try to elude these statements in such a way that the vigor of Christ's flesh communes with the body of believers, not by the presence of the substance of Christ's body and blood, but only by spirit. But Cyril clearly says that Christ is in us by natural participation, just as wax is mixed with melted wax. Likewise, he says that the body of natural life is joined to the corruptible nature of our body. And in Book 11, Treatises 26 & 27 on John, he says, "Since we consist of body and soul, we are joined with Christ in two ways: by a bodily union, in which He is bodily united to us with His body, as a Man, through the mystical benediction; and by a spiritual union, in which we receive the Holy Spirit and are united to God. And Christ is united to us as God, renewing our spirit by the grace of His Spirit to new life and participation in the divine nature."

Likewise, "Christ is the nexus, therefore, of our union with God the Father: having been naturally united to us, on the one hand, as Man; to God the Father, on the other hand, as God. For in bodily and substantially receiving the Son of God, who is united to the Father by nature, we are exalted and glorified, having been made partakers of the supreme nature." In his Epistle *ad Nestorium* and *in Declaratione Anathematismi*, 11, where he recites his confession of the doctrine of the Lord's Supper, Cyril affirms two things: **First**, the presence of the body and blood of the Lord, when he says, "That which is set forth in the Supper is the very body and blood of the vivifying Word." **Second**, he says that those who approach the mystical benedictions become partakers of the holy flesh and of the precious blood of Christ. Thus, what they receive is not common flesh, but as the truly vivifying flesh—the very flesh of the Word Himself. And he says that the articles of the resurrection of Christ and His assumption into heaven are not in conflict with this doctrine. But he says that he had set forth those things because Nestorius and those who thought like him were rashly trying to destroy the power of this mystery. He says the same thing in response to the objections of Theodoret: "Surely you are not pronouncing this Sacrament of ours to be cannibalism, irreverently urging the minds of those who have believed toward crass opinions, and attempting with human notions to treat those things which are grasped only by a pure and impenetrable faith?"

VII. At the time of **Damascenus**, who flourished about the year 700, it appears that struggles arose from those modes of speaking which were used by the more ancient writers. "The bread is a sign; the wine is a figure or symbol, etc." For from those phrases, some constructed the fanatical dogma, "As the bronze serpent and the showbread were figures of the body of Christ, and as the blood of a sheep in the Old Testament was a sign or symbol of the blood of Christ, so also the bread and wine of the Lord's Supper are only bare signs of the absent body and blood of Christ." Damascenus opposes that opinion, stirred up at his time, with these words in Book 4, ch. 14: "The bread and wine are not a figure of the body and blood of Christ. Far be it! But it is the very, deified body of the Lord, as the Lord Himself says, 'This is My body.' Not a *figure* of His body, but *His body*. And not a figure of His blood, but His blood. If you ask how it is present, we know nothing more than that the Word of the Lord ('This is My body') is true, and effective, and omnipotent; but the manner is inscrutable." Now, we should not hide the fact that Damascenus is guilty of other errors, such as the error concerning purgatory, the worship and adoration of images and relics. So while he attacks more vehemently that opinion which imagines the bare signs of the absent body and blood of the Lord in the Supper, he falters in that he spreads the not-obscure seeds of transubstantiation. Our faith, therefore, does not depend on the authority of Damascenus. But I merely note these things for the sake of the history; namely, that already at that time the conflicts were arising about the signs, figures, and symbols in the Lord's Supper, with which the presence of the body and blood of Christ was removed.

VIII. Eutropius places **Theophylact** at about the year 760. But since this Theophylact of whom we are now speaking received the surname "Bulgarius" from the Bulgarians when they were recently converted to the faith, the annotation of those who place him around the year 870 seems more likely. With great vehemence and in many places, he contends against that opinion which removes the substance of the body and blood of the Lord from the Supper, leaving only bare signs, leaving no doubt that the battles over the figurative interpretation of the words of the Supper which had begun to be stirred up at the time of Damascenus had grown significantly stronger by the time of Theophylact. He says about the 14th chapter of Mark: "'This is My body'—this, I say, which you are taking. For the bread is not merely some figure or representation of the Lord's body." But how is it, you ask, that the flesh is not seen? He responds that it is done for the sake of our infirmity, lest we shrink back in fear. On John 6, he says, "I am fully aware, however, that the bread which is eaten by us in the mysteries is not only some figuration of the Lord's body, but is the very flesh of the Lord. For He did not say, 'The bread which I will give is a figure of My flesh,' but 'is My flesh.'" On Matthew 26: "But in saying, 'This is My body,' He shows that the body itself is the bread which is consecrated on the altar, not a corresponding figure. For He did not say, 'This is a symbol,' but, 'This is My body,' demonstratively, lest anyone should think that those things which are seen are a type." But Theophylact also has some traces of transubstantiation which are sufficiently crass. For he says that the bread is "transformed, converted, and transelemented into the body of Christ," and indeed, in such a way that, when Christ walked on the earth, the bread was transmuted into His flesh by way of nourishment. Therefore, we do not learn from Theophylact the true doctrine of the Lord's Supper. But we note the historical narrative and observe what kinds of controversies existed at that time concerning the Lord's Supper. And we add this observation, that what Basil says about all arguments also occurred in this controversy, namely, "When farmers are zealous to straighten the crooked trunk of a tender tree, they err in the opposite direction by pulling too tightly."

IX. About the time of Charles the Bald, when some were insisting that the bread is only a figure of Christ's body, while others imagined such a "transformation (μεταποίησιν)", as Damascenus calls it, that not even the substance of bread remains behind, those conflicts which were stirred up under Damascenus and Theophylact began to lead to such a serious situation that even the emperor was disturbed by the clamor of the arguments. There a certain presbyter named Bertram wanted vehemently to refute that new dogma of transformation and transelementation (as it was called at that time, when the word "transubstantiation" was still unknown). He rightly says that there are two things in the Sacrament, one of which is seen, the other of which is believed. But in trying to avoid Charybdis, he fell into Scylla. For he works very hard to prove that there is an immense difference between the body of Christ which is given and received in the Supper and between that which was born of the Virgin Mary, nailed to a cross, dead, buried, and sitting at the right hand of the Father. But since he sees that the words of institution oppose him, he does not make much mention of this. He also says that the phrase "Christ's body" is attributed to the bread because of what it symbolizes, that, just as the substance of the visible bread nourishes the external man, so the Word of God, who is the Living Bread, or the Spirit of Christ, renews the minds of believers by partaking of Him. But Christ does not say, "This is the Word, the divinity, or My Spirit," but, "This is My body." Likewise He says, "The bread of the Eucharist is the body of Christ in no other way than that it is the body of the believing people. Moreover, just as the bread is the Church in a merely figurative and signifying way, in the same way it is also the body of Christ." But what will happen to the words of institution, "which is given for you"? Surely the Church was not also crucified for us, was it? So it is that when foolish men flee from vices, they run into the opposite vices. But this is how Bertram concludes his writing: "If these things are less than satisfying, let it be ascribed to our foolishness, which was less able to explain what it wished to express." Therefore, that doctrine of Bertram was not used or received in the Church at that time.

X. At the same time, Johannes Scotus, the Benedictine monk (not the famous *Sententiarius*, but much more ancient) had great authority because of his learning. After the emperor had summoned him to France from England, where the University of Oxford had recently been established, he translated the books of Dionysius into Latin. He also wrote about the Lord's Supper, but his books are not extant, as far as I know. But Lanfranc reports that Berengar had affirmed that he had drawn the seeds of his own opinion from the writings of that Scotus. It is not difficult, therefore, to deduce what Scotus' understanding was of the Lord's Supper.

The histories tell, moreover, that while Scotus was presenting and defending his opinion publicly in an auditorium, he was first blinded, then impaled by his students' writing utensils. Therefore, that form of doctrine about the Lord's Supper which Bertram and Scotus describe was not common and accepted at that time, but was considered a new and fanatical dogma, which was at odds with the sound and ancient faith. And so, at that time, God wondrously suppressed that unfortunate contention.

XI. Trithenius notes that **Paschasius**, whose writing on the Lord's Supper is still extant, flourished about the year 880. So it appears that Bertram, Scotus, and Paschasius lived at the same time, and thus Paschasius wrote specifically against the corruptions of Bertram and Scotus, if the extant writings are compared. It is useful to observe what the chief points of contention were at that time on which the controversy over the Lord's Supper hinged. But since we cannot determine these from the histories of that time, which are woefully incomplete, they must be gathered from the writings of the authors themselves. I will note, therefore, the chief points which demonstrate that the conflicts at that time were very similar to those which are stirred up in our time. **First**, it has already been shown in the preceding pages that they had begun at that time to argue over transubstantiation. That argument, therefore, occasioned some to remove the substance of the bread from the Supper, while others removed the substance of Christ's body and blood. Paschasius says that there are two things present in the Sacrament, according to the words of institution, namely, the visible and perceptible substance, that is, the elements of bread and wine; and, under that visible appearance, the body and blood of Christ are present, which are not sensed by sight and taste, but by faith are understood from the Word to be present. And although he fights rather weakly against transubstantiation, he clearly says that a sacramental conversion takes place, without any discoloration of the substance of the bread and wine. And Gabriel Biel cites certain words from Paschasius with which he rejected the reservation, storage, and parading around of the Sacrament on this basis, since Christ gave the disciples His body, not to store it away or to carry it around, but to use it as He instituted it, saying, "Take, eat."

Second, we noted earlier that the battles were stirred up at that time concerning those modes of speaking—that the bread is a figure, sign, symbol, mystery, etc.—and some were making much of the "signs" in order to remove the substance of Christ's body from the Supper, while others were fighting so strenuously against the figures that they introduced transelementation. But Paschasius says that, since it is a Sacrament, we cannot deny that the bread is a figure, since antiquity spoke in that way. But what we must ask is, in what way is it a figure? Not because it is a sign of something that is absent, as the manna and the water from the rock signified the future incarnation of Christ. But it is a figure because, in the visible thing, through the bodily appearance, and under the cover of visible things, something more is understood from the word to be present which is not sensed by sight and taste, namely, the flesh and blood of the Lord.

Third, since Bertram presses that argument about the similarity of the Sacraments of the Old and New Testaments, Paschasius posits and demonstrates the difference between the manna and the bread of the Lord's Supper; namely, that the figures of the Old

Testament were shadows, while the Eucharist has the associated truth, since Christ says, "This is My body."

Fourth, he affirms that no other flesh is given and received in the Supper than that which was born of the Virgin Mary, suffered on the cross, and rose from the dead. And since Bertram taught the opposite, Paschasius often repeats: "That which once flowed from Christ's side, believers now drink in the chalice." Likewise: "The true and real flesh of Christ is truly and really received." Likewise: "The body of Christ is contained in a present manner under the bread, and the blood under the figure of the wine." He also says: "The flesh of Christ is really extended to us by His own hand through the hand of the minister." He sets these things against Bertram, who imagined that the body of Christ is merely present and received in a figurative and signifying way.

Fifth, since many people were disturbed by Bertram's and Scotus' equivocation of terms (bodily, carnally, and spiritually), Paschasius presents an explanation. Since the presence of Christ's body is not perceived by any sense of reason, nor is it present in a carnal way according to the thinking of reason, nor is it eaten like common food which is converted into our flesh and blood, in this sense he grants that it is rightly said to be present, not carnally, but spiritually. Likewise, since Christ's body in the Supper is not seen or touched, he says that, in this sense, the body can be called spiritual, as Paul also says in 1 Cor. 15, as long as it is understood to be the true and real body. These things he sets against Bertram, as we noted above.

Sixth, these, too, are his words. "It is not as some imagine, that the soul alone is fed by this mystery, since the soul alone is not saved by the death of Christ, but also our flesh. Through this mystery our flesh is renewed, flesh for flesh, to immortality and incorruptibility. It is spiritually united and transformed, so that the very substance of Christ is found in our flesh, even as we know that He Himself also assumed our flesh in His deity." Likewise, "Through the Sacrament of His body and blood, Christ is shown to abide in us, not only by faith, but also by the unity of flesh and blood, and for this reason we, the members of Christ, are now fed by His flesh, so that we are found to be nothing other than His body, from whence we live, and His blood."

Seventh, he also rejects the notion of Capernaitic eating, that is, the Scythian butchering of the flesh of Christ in the Supper. For he says, "Although the flesh of Christ is consumed every day, He Himself remains the living and uninjured Lamb. For 'He does not die; death no longer has dominion over Him.'" Likewise, "Christ is not torn to pieces by the teeth in the eating of the Sacrament." And he rejects by name the canons which are still to this day tossed about by the Papists under the name of Clement, namely, that "one must take into account the excrement, if the appearances are still supposedly able to be discerned." Likewise, "One should not eat common food within six hours of receiving the Sacrament, lest the foods be mixed together." These he calls "frivolous, apocryphal works."

Eighth, he also recalls that the false claim was made at that time concerning local inclusion. Likewise, he also responds simply to the question of whether the body of Christ is called down from heaven in order that He may be present in the Supper. "Free rein should not be given to reason concerning the miracle of this Sacrament, so that it should anxiously twist itself into knots as to how in fact Christ's body is able to be contained in a present way (*praesentialiter*) under the appearance of bread and His blood under the figure of wine." Likewise: "Although He said only once, 'Let the earth produce,' and yet still today all things are created from that word, so also He has commanded His body and blood to be present in this commemoration, and what He orders is done. If a person does not believe these things, he is worse than an unbeliever. For that one cannot approve what he has not learned; and this one does not believe that what he has acknowledged to be done in many things contrary to nature is done in the flesh of Christ."

XII. After nearly two hundred years, in A.D. 1050, the Sacramentarian controversy was rekindled much more vehemently than before by the Frenchman Berengar. The story of that conflict has been described by many. We will briefly note the chief points. Now, the Berengarian controversy was not principally about transubstantiation (however much that was added later); it was about the true presence of the body and blood of the Lord in the Supper. After two writings were set forth concerning the Lord's Supper, of which one was by Scotus, the other by Paschasius, Berengar professed that he had learned his understanding of the Eucharist from Scotus, while he rejected and condemned the understanding of Paschasius. We explained Paschasius' understanding above.

But the histories record that the testimony of antiquity was opposed to Berengar in his disputation, based on Augustine, who writes this on the statements of Prosper: "This is what we say, that in all ways we strive to prove that the Eucharist is composed of two things, that it consists of two things: the visible appearance of the elements and the invisible flesh and blood of our Lord Jesus Christ, of the Sacrament and the essence of the Sacrament (*re sacramenti*), that is, the body and blood of Christ, just as the person of Christ consists and is made up of God and Man, since Christ is God and Man. For everything contains in itself the nature and the truth of those things of which it is composed."

It is said, moreover, that Berengar responded that he "concedes, indeed, both the Sacrament and the essence of the Sacrament. But the essence of the Sacrament is present only in sign and figure, not in reality." And he added the following proof: "If the body of Christ were really present in the Eucharist, then He would surely have to be visible there, since it is written about the body of Christ, 'Touch and see!' But now, having been raised up into heaven where He sits at the right hand of the Father until the times of the restoration of all things, He cannot be called down from heaven." The histories report that these were the words of Berengar. They also note with these words the forms of speech which he used: "The body of Christ is not really present in the Eucharist, but only in sign." Likewise, "The bread is not the true body of Christ, but only a figure of it."

But for the sake of the present conflicts, we should not pass over this: In the first revocation, Berengar retracted one of his sayings; namely, that the bread in the Lord's Supper is only a bare sign and figure of the absent body of Christ. But later, although he retained the original statement about the absence of the substance of the Lord's body and blood in the Supper, he began to speak differently and more mildly and preached many things magnificently about the power and efficacy of Christ's body. Indeed, Lanfranc recalls that after the first revocation, Berengar renewed the conflict, but he does not express what the arguments were.

However, from Berengar's second revocation, which Sabellicus places in his *Enneades*, one can clearly note what I said about power and efficacy. This, among other things, is included in that second revocation: "With the heart I believe and with the mouth I confess that the bread and wine are the true body of Christ, which hung on the cross and sits at the right hand of the Father, and the true blood which flowed from His side, not merely by way of sign and the power of the Sacrament, but in property of nature and truth of substance."

Furthermore, in the Berengarian conflict, it was not only the question of the presence of Christ's body that was disputed, but also the question of transubstantiation, which had been invented not long before, but at that time it was established by the authority of the popes with very crass words concerning the sensuality of the presence of Christ's body. But since that figment conflicts with the Word of God and with purer antiquity, we freely reject and condemn it, as demonstrated above in the confessions of our churches.

We have recounted these things about Berengar only for the sake of history, insofar as it bears some similarity to the conflicts of our time, not because we approve each and every decree of the Council of Vercelli.

Finally, it is worthwhile to observe carefully what is written about Berengar's death. For when, on January 6th, he sensed that the hour of his death was imminent, it is written that he sighed and said, "Today the Lord Jesus Christ will appear to me for my salvation, as I hope, on account of repentance, or for my harsh condemnation, as I fear, on account of those men whom I was unable to lead back to the right way after they were deceived by perverse doctrine." This miserable example shows sufficiently how much danger one plays with by fabricating opinions in this matter.

XIII. Then, over three hundred years later, Wycliffe in England began to defend and to propagate the same error in both preaching and writing. He used these forms of speech: "Christ is not really present in the Eucharist—not with a proper, bodily presence." But as John was Elijah figuratively, not personally, so the bread is the body of Christ figuratively. For he says, "Without any ambiguity the saying, 'This is My body,' is figurative, just like that saying, 'John is Elijah.'" It is noteworthy that John Hus, who was in the habit of reading Wycliffe's books, embraced his doctrine in many articles, since he saw that Wycliffe rejected the fiction about transubstantiation in the doctrine of the Eucharist, as well as the mutilation of the second kind, as they call it. He, too, rejected these things, for he saw what the testimonies of Scripture were. But he did not approve of Wycliffe's denial of the true presence of Christ's body in the Supper, for he saw that this teaching conflicted with the words of institution, as those who follow Hus' doctrine affirm.

XIV. The **Waldensians** presented to King Vladislaus a confession of their doctrine around A.D. 1506 which still exists in printed form. And in the article on the Lord's Supper, after having accumulated many statements about Christ's ascension and about

His going away to the Father, they conclude at length that, "After His ascension, before the Last Day, Christ is not on earth personally and bodily with His natural body, but is in a single place at the right hand of God, and thus the bread is the body of Christ as John was Elijah, since it contradicts the Gospel to point to Christ as being here or there." These words, among others, are extant in their confession. But in the year 1523, before the conflict with Carlstadt arose, after they had sent their confession to Luther for him to evaluate, they were admonished by him in a friendly way about the errors in that article in a writing that still exists. And afterwards, when the Zwinglians were seeking support for their opinion in the doctrine of the Waldensians after the Waldensian confession had been published, the Waldensians publicly testified in a repetition and clarification of their confession that they approved Luther's understanding of the Lord's Supper as being harmonious with the Word of God and that they disagreed with Zwingli.

Finally, Carlstadt, with his little books, was the first in our time to publicly scatter the sparks from whence that most grievous Sacramentarian flame blazed up, which still burns in the Church and causes terrible groaning among the godly and a plausible offense among the Papists. For when, in Luther's absence in A.D. 1522, Carlstadt had seditiously stirred up many problems in the Church at Wittenberg and had incited the people to violently remove the statues from the temples, contending that the civil law should be condemned and that the Law of Moses should be brought back into play, together with other fanatical opinions, he was sharply rebuked by Luther, and his seditious actions were condemned. Therefore, inflamed with a desire for revenge, he left Wittenberg and joined himself to those fanatics who pretended to have visions and conversations with God. Indeed, in his preaching among his own followers, he gnawed away at part of the doctrine of the Lord's Supper. But when Luther was sent to Jena by the Duke of Saxony in order to extinguish the fire before it spread, there Carlstadt gave Luther the middle finger and boasted that he paid no attention to Luther, that Luther's highest erudition was merely to preach about faith and love, that he both would and could defend his own opinion about the Lord's Supper in public writings. Thus, in 1524, having published his little books in Basel, Carlstadt disseminated his opinion of the Lord's Supper into the world. And this was his chief principle: Since the demonstrative pronoun ("this") does not agree in gender with the preceding noun ("bread"), therefore Christ only gave His disciples bread, and they received and ate nothing but bare bread. But after a certain interval of time, Christ pointed to His body, which was reclining at the table, and said, "This is My body which is given for you." Furthermore, Carlstadt revealed to his followers that a certain man had revealed this to him: Since there is a period after the word "eat," and since the next statement begins with a capital letter, "This is My body," it does not go with the preceding words.

Luther responded at the beginning of the following year and inscribed his book with this title: *Against those who boast that they have the heavenly breath, so that they are able, like Prophets, to set up new dogmas without the certain testimony of Scripture*. Therefore, after the die had been cast in this way by Carlstadt, and it seemed to him that this was the quickest way to overturn the trafficking of Masses, namely, to teach that only bare bread and wine are present in the Supper, there followed that fateful and calamitous year, 1525. For in that year, the pope publicly promulgated his blasphemous marketing of the Year of Jubilee. In that year, the Sacramentarian disputations were reaching their climax. And early in the same year followed the bloody tumults of sedition.

Therefore, since the minds of the common people seemed to be inclined toward any change whatsoever, **Zwingli**, who had long been nursing in private the monstrosity of the Sacramentarian opinion, stepped into the arena. This is what he writes about himself: "For more years than it is now convenient to say we were of this opinion concerning the Eucharist." Likewise: "No one among us ever truly believed that in this bread he was eating any such thing which we have dreamed." But he notes that most people, who did not disapprove of the summary of Carlstadt's understanding about the absence of the Lord's body and blood in the Supper, were nevertheless deterred by the violent and too-rigid exposition of the words of the Supper which Carlstadt alleged. Therefore, he imagined how with another more plausible color he might bring back into the theater the fable that had practically been driven off stage, which, nevertheless, he noticed was pleasing to many, because it takes neither great faith nor great effort to believe that bread is bread. At first, he began to test the minds of men with his sermons. Then, he began to press the matter with a certain letter, written privately to a certain Reutlingen man in such a way that he might spread it among many. And since he noticed that no pursuits of theater were lacking to him, either manifest or hidden, he finally appeared publicly with his commentary at the spring market of Frankfurt, disputing with many that in the statement, "This is My body," the linking verb "is" must be explained as "signifies," so that the representation of the bread signifies the absent body of Christ. And he boasted that he had discovered this new gem in the epistle of a certain Batavus.

The history which Zwingli himself recounts is worth remembering among future generations, for from it one can judge by what spirit that conflict was stirred up, with how dubious and how anxious a conscience it was undertaken. This is how he writes. Soon after his commentary was published, when he was standing before the senate trying to abrogate the Mass and to institute his own new synaxis, he writes that a certain scribe opposed him sharply with this as his chief argument: that Zwingli was departing from the clear character of the words and was not proving with sufficient certainty or clarity that the word "is" in the words of the Supper should be taken as "signifies." Indeed, his examples from Luke 8, "The seed is the Word of God," and from Mat. 13, "The field is the world," were very dissimilar. For there the parables come first, and their explanation is given with the word "is." But in the Lord's Supper, it is not at all that way. Zwingli was so disturbed by this objection that, although he said something at that moment, lest he should seem to be entirely silent, he felt the prick of a raging conscience. He himself tells it with these words: "After we had withdrawn from the senate, we began to ponder all things, to contemplate all things, namely, where we could uncover examples which would not be linked to any parable. But no examples were found other than those which were included in the commentary or those which were similar to these. But when the 13th day was approaching (the words I am telling are true, so true that the conscience compels the one who wants to hide them to pour out what the Lord has communicated, being not unaware that I am exposing myself to all sorts of insults and mockery)—when, I say, the light of April 13th was approaching, it seemed to me I was in a dream, that I was wearily contending again with my adversary, the scribe, and that I lost my voice, so that, although I knew the truth, my tongue denied its benefit and I was unable to speak. This inability to speak (as dreams are sometimes accustomed to play deceptively at night, for we are speaking of nothing higher than a dream, as it pertains to us, although what we have learned through a dream is not a trivial thing, thank God, for whose glory alone we publish these things) seemed to disturb me greatly. There seemed to appear *ex machina* a guide (whether he was black or white I do not recall, for I am telling a dream) who said, 'Why do you not simply give him for an answer what is written in Exodus 12? "For it is the Lord's Passover." Immediately after seeing this specter, I leap out of bed and immediately look up the passage in the Septuagint, and then I discuss it courageously before the whole assembly.'" Thus far Zwingli.

Now, after Zwingli had brought out the full regimen of his arguments, together with his reinforcements and reserves, his sycophants and allies were afraid that Zwingli's authority would not be sufficient for such a perilous battle, especially among outsiders. Therefore, since **Oecolampadius** had indicated a number of times in front of the assembly that Zwingli's understanding was not displeasing to him, they prevailed upon him somehow, both those who were present and those who were absent, to send out reinforcements to aid Zwingli's fearful army. And so, within a few months, Oecolampadius embellishes that tragedy with more erudition and more splendor, having cleverly amassed many different statements of the ancients, contending that the word "body" in the words of the Supper should be understood, not as the substance of Christ's flesh, but as a figure of His absent body. And since Oecolampadius had great authority among the learned on account of his singular erudition and temperate life, he seemed poised to make no small impact, especially since the chief doctors in neighboring Swabia were joined to him in a very close friendship, to such a degree that the majority had used him as an instructor, leading him to dedicate his book to them. But the Swabian doctors came together in agreement rather quickly and, in a well-reasoned written response, rejected and refuted the conclusion of Oecolampadius.

There came on the scene a third main character, who, by various writings here and there, was successful in moving everyone either to openly agree with Oecolampadius, or, if they could not, to simply withhold their opinion, but in such a way that they did not defame Oecolampadius or portray him as thinking improperly about the Lord's Supper. For, with these words, he himself recounts in a certain apology the argument of the letter. "At the same time, in the name of the Church in Strasbourg, Chaselius was also sent to Wittenberg with these mandates: to explain how dangerous was the blaze that would be kindled if those who were rightly and completely united, in mind and zeal, in assaulting the idols of the papal realm, were to clash with one another in hostile writings. He predicted, in addition, that the authority to teach among those who professed the Sacramentarian opinion, would be diminished, for it did not seem to come from the cause of the Church. Therefore, he reported that it seemed advisable that the faithful should be dissuaded from asking about the presence of the body and blood of the Lord and should be trained simply with the word and faith." These things were instituted with this plan in mind, that Luther should either be softened (for his silence was clearly being sought), or at least that his pen, whose attack they feared, should be blunted by that very delay. But there is no need to report Luther's response to Chaselius, for it resides in the public record.

In the same year (1525), Carlstadt, who had been the primary author of this conflict, wrote to Luther that the things he had published concerning the Lord's Supper he had written, not for the sake of defining, but for the sake of disputing, and for the sake of rooting out the truth. Therefore, since Luther saw that Carlstadt had doubts about his own opinion, and that the rest of them, as he had understood from Chaselius, were hesitant, he did not at that time immediately prepare a just refutation of the arguments of Zwingli and Oecolampadius with a lengthy writing. But in a letter which he published, written to the Church in Strasbourg, and in a preface which he attached to the written document of the Swabians, he publicly testified that he disagreed with the Sacramentarian opinion with all his heart and referred to his own book, which he had written against Carlstadt, in which he had already explained and confirmed in a rather lengthy manner his own understanding of the Lord's Supper. He did the same thing considerably more sharply in his sermon about the Lord's Supper against the fanatics. To this, Zwingli, with great confidence, as if he were already certain of victory, responded at length with his own exegesis, reemphasizing those words about God being "impanated, edible, cooked, roasted, baked, etc." Meanwhile, the remaining Zwinglian allies in this battle were insidiously spreading the venom of the Sacramentarian opinion in the books of others, under the guise of translation, as, for example, in Luther's *Postil* and in Pomeranus' *Psalter*. They also appealed to other doctors in Wittenberg, as if they were not averse to the Zwinglian opinion. This is what caused Luther finally to respond more vehemently in the year 1527.

But that conflict was instigated in various ways after Carlstadt, Zwingli, and Oecolampadius—by the rest of their associates. For some would invert the word order: "My body which is given for you is this, namely, bread, that is, food for the soul." Others in this way: "What is given for you, this is My body." There were those who mangled the context like this: "This is My body, in remembrance of Me, that is, a memorial sign of My absent body."

But in the year 1529, since, in the meeting at Speyer, the Papists seemed to be about to condemn the cause of the Gospel with unjust prejudice—and that, with a not implausible appearance, on account of those violent clashes over the Lord's Supper—and were already writing harsh edicts, therefore a plan was formed in the same place by those who had given their names to the renewed ecclesiastical doctrine that it was better that in this affair several good men should come together in colloquy. And in this way the **Marburg Colloquy** was instituted, the acts of which have been described by Philip Melanchthon and are extant in the fourth volume in German at Jena. After that colloquy, when the Augsburg Confession of the Faith was presented to Emperor Charles in the year 1530, the cities which had received and accepted the Zwinglian understanding of the Lord's Supper were not allowed to subscribe; instead, they offered the emperor their own writing. In 1531, Zwingli fell in battle on October 11th. One month later, Oecolampadius also died, as he was unable to bear the heartache he felt from Zwingli's violent end.

But Carlstadt survived them both. Since, by his own subterfuge and with Luther's intercession, he had again crept into the grace of the Elector of Saxony, he remained in private for several years in the little town of Kemberg, where he busied himself with chopping wood, selling cakes, and similar things of that sort. During that time, Luther dealt with him, trying to call him away from his error, as recorded in the fourth volume. Finally, he snuck away in secret and was made Archdeacon of the Church at Zürich. He later went to Basel, and there he finished his life in the ecclesiastical ministry. There is a letter that tells of his death; I will include some of its words here. The churchmen of Basel write that Carlstadt was a venomous plague to his own church and that he was killed by the devil. They write that there appeared to him, while he was preaching, a large man who entered the temple, stood next to a certain magistrate, and then left the temple again and entered Carlstadt's home. There, finding his son alone, he lifted him up in his hands as if he would dash him to the ground. But he left him uninjured and ordered him to tell his father that he would come back after three days and would bear him away. That is also what happened. For the boy was stricken with sudden terrors and died after three days. Carlstadt had asked the magistrate after the sermon who that large man was. The magistrate answered that he had seen no one, etc.

The protagonists of this conflict, Zwingli and Oecolampadius, had finally been removed from the scene, but it had been agreed at the Marburg Colloquy that both sides would refrain from too severe a pen. Therefore, among the Zwinglians, although in their own churches, in their teaching, they rabidly retained their former opinion of the Sacrament, nevertheless in their public writings there was either great silence on the part of some, or in other cases much gentler voices were being heard. The majority were looking for flexible stage shoes, seeking a feigned and insidious reconciliation. Indeed, this caused a much more dangerous Sacramentarian conflict than there had been before, as if the disagreement were a matter of words rather than with the actual understanding, even as the matter is also handled with the same cunning at the present time. It is helpful in this case to note those histories, so that the traps may be recognized and avoided.

In the year 1532, Luther was forced for this very reason to write to the Duke of Prussia that he should not, because of this outward appearance, allow himself to be persuaded either to admit or to tolerate such fanatical spirits in his territory.

In the following year, he wrote a public letter to the people of Frankfurt, opposing those two-tongued Sacramentarians who, in their manners of speaking, invented such stage shoes that both sides could wear them, so that both sides, using the same words, retained and hid different and, indeed, conflicting opinions. In truth, many who were not forewarned were being deceived by this fraud; they did not suspect that anything was amiss, because they were hearing the same forms of speech. But in 1535, the people of Zürich (as they themselves tell the story) had decided to break their silence and publicly renew the conflict, setting aside their former pretense. But Capito went and dissuaded them from it, using this as his chief argument: That by maintaining the pretense, it seemed possible to come together in concord.

At the beginning of the year 1536, the Swiss had assembled at Basel and were about to repeat the confession of their faith. Capito and Bucer also came there and, with a lengthy speech, showed them how much toil it had cost them to establish concord between Luther and the Zwinglians and that the matter had already been going on for some time. Therefore, with all their might they begged them to omit from the article of the Lord's Supper those words which had caused the substance of the disagreement up to that point and to temper and moderate their confession in such a way that it might promote concord (namely, as shown later by the outcome, that they might retain their original opinion and, under the guise of concord, be enabled to profit further from their deceit). This, then, is how the Swiss at that time explained the article of the Lord's Supper: "This is how we teach about the mystical Supper, that the Lord truly offers His body and blood—that is, Himself—to His people in order that He may live in them more and more, and they in Him. Not that the Lord's body and blood are naturally united with the bread and wine, or locally included in it, or considered here with any sort of carnal presence, but that the bread and wine are symbols by which the true communion of His body and blood is given by the Lord Himself, through the ministry of the Church, not for food that perishes in the stomach, but for the nourishment of eternal life, etc."

These things must be carefully observed, because those stage shoes are now being displayed in the same matter with practically the same words.

In the same year, 1536, Bucer went with his followers to Wittenberg, and on May 29th, the Formula of Concord[4] was established in the Sacramentarian matter, which we recounted above. The churches of northern Germany accepted it. But the Swiss were unwilling to subscribe, for two reasons (as they themselves recall). First, because it had been written in the Formula of Concord that the Lord's body and blood are truly and substantially present, given, and received with the bread and wine. Second, because it said there that Christ's body and blood are truly offered even to the unworthy, and that the unworthy receive it, where the words and institution of Christ are preserved.

But Bucer presented a lengthy clarification, the sum of which was to allow the Swiss to be able to accept and understand that Formula of Concord in the same way as they had stated the matter in their own article at Basel. Therefore, in the same year, the magistrate of Zürich wrote to Luther as if it were now merely a question of the mode of presence—whether Christ's body descends from heaven into the bread (since the article of faith says that He will not descend before the Last Day), or whether it is an earthly and carnal presence. Luther responded to this letter in 1537 in a friendly manner as one who hoped that concord would easily be achieved, if it were merely a question of the mode of presence. We recounted in the beginning the words of his response. Indeed, these words seemed to have an outward form of true concord and

4 That is, the Wittenberg Concord.

confession. But meanwhile, the Swiss were proceeding in their own churches, teaching about the Lord's Supper as they had before, and they were bringing to light the works of Zwingli with new excuses.

Schwenckfeldt was also boasting that he and the remaining Zwinglians, who thoroughly retained their original understanding, were in great agreement with Luther in the Sacramentarian matter.

For these and other reasons, Luther was moved in 1544 to publish his final confession on the Lord's Supper, mainly for this purpose: Lest anyone should attempt after his death to persuade the world, under the pretext of the Marburg Colloquy or this Formula of Concord, that Luther, in the end, either approved of the Zwinglians' opinion, or at least that no terrible disagreement existed between them, even though there was some discrepancy over the article of the Lord's Supper. We can now judge that this was all done entirely by divine providence. For if that final confession of his had not been published, not all of his writings together could defend Luther from being labeled a Zwinglian, even if unwillingly so. For all can see how that conflict has broken open again after Luther's death and with what artifices and skill it is being fought. Indeed, this is why I have collected these historical notes. For they can inform our judgment in the present conflicts on account of their similarities.

Now may the Son of God, our Lord Jesus Christ, who instituted His Holy Supper that it might be a bond of mutual love and fellowship, preserve by His Spirit the minds of those who teach and of those who learn, and may He turn them toward godly and salutary concord.

Amen.

XXXII. The doctrine of the common participation of the properties of the two natures in the person of Christ.

The use of this doctrine in the Church is very great and necessary. For in Matthew 16, Christ says that the Rock on which He would build His Church is the confession that the Son of Man is the Son of God. This is the very doctrine of the *communicatio idiomatum*—the common participation of properties. Hardly any controversy was stirred up in the Church as difficult as the Nestorian controversy or the Eutychian controversy or any of the rest that dealt with the common participation of properties. For nearly 300 years, the Church was continually and not trivially plagued by those conflicts. Indeed, the ecumenical Council of Ephesus, the fifth Council of Chalcedon, and then the sixth, deal with practically nothing other than the history of those conflicts. Now, among those disturbances, when the most learned men in the Church were wrestling among themselves concerning this doctrine, God, in a special act of kindness, raised up the most excellent man, **Cyril**, whom He rendered suitable, by His Spirit, for elucidating and explaining this controversy. Because of his vigilance and toil, we have the doctrine of the common participation of properties as it is established from the foundations of Scripture in a manageable and agreeable form. **Damascenus**, too, did admirable work in this matter, and from him they later took up many useful rules in the schools. But Luther, both elsewhere and especially in his little book, *De ultimis verbis Davidis* and in *De Conciliis et Ecclesia*, explained this doctrine with unique skill and clarity.

For my own private use, I have selected from these lengthier writings certain rules with which, in my opinion, the chief part of this doctrine can be grasped in the simplest way. It is quite clear that the doctrine itself has been carefully treated by the more ancient writers. But quarrels have arisen in our time concerning the title of this article, for the phrase "common participation of properties" is not found even among the more recent writers like Lombard, who, nevertheless, expressly treats this doctrine in Book 3. Damascenus, Bk. 3, ch. 4, calls it an "exchange" (ἀντίδοσις), and more frequently an "alternation" (ἀλλοίωσις), having taken up the term that was in use at that time in the grammar schools. For that figure of speech which we now call "interchange" (ἑτέρωσις), when one part of a speech is substituted and used for the other, the more ancient grammarians called "alternation" (ἀλλοίωσις). This term was more pleasing to Zwingli, for it was more accommodating to his principle, since he pretended that there was an alternation in John 6, that the word "flesh" was to be understood as "the divine nature." In the same way, others imagined that, in that saying in 1 John 1, "the blood of Jesus Christ cleanses us from all sin," the word "blood" is to be understood as "divinity." Therefore, the term "alternation" was more pleasing to them. However, beyond all controversy the term "common participation of properties" (κοινωνία ἰδιωμάτων) is both clearer and more suitable, as the treatise itself will demonstrate. For there is not merely a relationship of properties (*relatio idiomatum*), as Paul refers to his sufferings as "the sufferings of Christ," Col. 1, but a common participation. Nor is it a confusion, but a common participation of properties. It is quite clear that the Scholastics did not invent this term, because, of course, it is undoubtedly a Greek phrase, κοινωνία ἰδιωμάτων, and it is not unknown that the schools at that time were practically inundated with Greek letters. Therefore, it was undoubtedly taken from a sermon of the ancient Church. For when the ancients describe the error of Nestorius, they speak in this way: That Nestorius had identified two natures in Christ, but that they have no common participation with one another (*verum* ἀκοινωνήτους).

Cyril often divides the entire doctrine into the appropriation (ἰδιοποιΐα) and impartation (κοινοποιΐα) of properties. At the Council of Chalcedon, the epistle of Leo was read, stating that the Latin Church speaks in this way: "Each nature works what is proper to it, with the common participation of the other (*cum communicatione alterius*)." Those from Illyricum and Palestine began to take issue with that mode of speaking, but it was shown that Cyril had also spoken in this way and had said these things about the term. Therefore, we retain the customary term, which is both helpful and clear. For the *allœosis* of Zwingli also corrupted the matter itself by the changing of the term. But for the sake of orderly teaching, we will divide the doctrine of the common participation of properties into three classes (*genera*), for this is practically how Cyril and Damascenus divide it.

THE FIRST CLASS
of properties which belong to the natures.

This definition is given: The common participation of properties[5] is the predication in which the property which corresponds to one nature is attributed concretely to the person.

This definition summarily embraces the entire doctrine, but for the sake of clarification, certain other rules are added.

However, the foundation of this entire doctrine consists in these two axioms:

First, the distinction between the natures must be maintained, for in this way the properties of the divine and human nature are distinguished.

Second, the unity of the person must be preserved, for in this way the common participation of properties takes place in the person.

Samosatene, with his followers, conceded, at least, that there are two natures in Christ, but claimed that they are not shared

5 *communicatio idiomatum*, lit. the communication of properties or attributes.

with one another (ἀκοινωνήτους), as Suidas notes. In other words, there is no common participation of properties.

This, then, is the true and uninterrupted understanding of the Church: In the incarnate Christ, there are and remain two natures, whole and distinct, united without confusion or conversion, so that each one retains its own properties. According to that very ancient saying, popular also with Origen and, indeed, with the even earlier Justin, "What He was, that He has remained; and what He was not, that He has assumed." The Church defended this statement at the Council of Chalcedon against Eutyches, who, after removing the distinction between the natures, utterly denied that some properties in the person of Christ belong to the divine nature, while others belong to the human.

Moreover, those two whole and distinct natures have been united in such a way that, in the incarnate Christ, the divine and human nature is one person. For the Scripture proclaims one Christ, one Son, one Lord, not two.

The Church condemned this error in Nestorius, that he also attributed two persons to the two natures in Christ. For he contended that the properties of the divine nature are to be attributed to Christ the God, not the Man. And, on the other hand, the attributes of the human nature are to be attributed to Christ the Man, not Christ the God.

From these foundations arises the doctrine of the common participation of properties. For since the natures have not been confused, the properties of each one remain intact. And since one person is God and Man, therefore, as the natures are united into one person, so also the things predicated of the natures are attributed to the one person, so that what is proper to the human nature is attributed to the Son of God, and what is proper to the divine nature, in turn, is attributed to the Son of Man. For whatever He does as God, it cannot be denied that He does also as Man, since "God is the Man," as Augustine says. And that predication is called the common participation of properties.

Nicephorus, Bk. 18, ch. 52, *Contra Severum*, writes thus: "The Catholic Church professes our Lord Jesus Christ, that the substance consists of two natures, of Deity, I say, and of humanity, in such a way that each of these natures, after the union, preserves its own properties intact; and that the union of these two natures admits no mixture or confusion, no mutation or alteration. Eutyches has imagined that the two natures, after the union, have undergone a mixture, so that the divinity suffered the things which were of the humanity, and vice versa." The words of Nicephorus.

Evagrius[6], Bk. 2, ch. 4 of his history, reveals the same understanding: "By no means do we remove the distinction between the natures on account of the union. Rather, the property of each nature is preserved intact, having come together into one person, etc." This is where the customary form of speaking comes from: "With the property of each nature intact and preserved."

Therefore, we must firmly maintain that the divine nature neither becomes, nor is said to be, the human nature on account of the union, or vice versa. For the natures both are, and remain, distinct. But since a union has been made in the person of the Word in such a way that there is now one person consisting of both natures, therefore, whether He is called the Son of God or the Son of Man, God or Man, not only the one nature is understood, either divine or human, but the person who subsists in both the divine and human nature. For the divinity dwells in Christ, not by assistance or by association—as Paul says of himself in 1 Tim. 4, "The Lord assisted me and comforted me"—but bodily, that is, so that there is one person together with the human nature. And "the force of that union is so great," says Bernard, "that God and man are truly and mutually

6 Evagrius Scholasticus (A.D. 536–594), known for his six volume history of the Church, not to be confused with the mystical theologian, Evagrius Ponticus.

predicated of Him."

From this there arose a useful rule in the schools: The concrete names do not designate only the one nature, but the whole person, who subsists in both natures. Thus the Scholastics say, "The concrete names stand for the person, not for the natures."

This rule has been drawn from manifest testimonies of Scripture and is very useful. Matthew 16: "The Son of Man is the Son of the living God." John 6: "If you see the Son of Man ascend to where He was before." 1 Cor. 15: "The second man from heaven." Here the concrete names, taken from His humanity, do not designate only the human nature, for that nature was not begotten from the essence of the Father, nor was it in heaven before the incarnation; instead, they designate the person, in whom there is both a divine and a human nature. Thus in 1 Cor. 2: "The Lord of glory has been crucified." Acts 20: "God has purchased the Church with His own blood." Here the divine names, taken from the divinity, do not only signify the divine nature, for that nature has no blood. No, it signifies the person as He subsists in both natures.

From this brief summary, many things can be neatly settled. Some, based on that passage from 1 Timothy 2, "The man Jesus Christ is the Mediator," want to infer that the human nature alone is the Mediator. Osiander, based on the passage from Jer. 23, "Jehovah our righteousness," and from Mat. 6, "His righteousness," concludes that the divine nature alone is our righteousness. But the concrete names, whether of the divine or of the human nature, do not stand for the nature, either divine or human, but for the person. Thus in 1 Tim. 2, "the man" does not signify the human nature alone. And in Jer. 23, "Jehovah" does not signify the divine nature abstractly, but that person in whom there are two natures, the divine and the human.

It is usually said that these propositions are true through the common participation of properties. That should be understood in this way: Since there is one person subsisting in two natures, therefore also the things which fit with only one nature are attributed to the person concretely. It is not necessary that the things which are predicated of the person in this class fit with both natures, but it is sufficient if they fit according to the one, either divine or human.

For, as Cyril reports in Epistle 29, Arius wanted the flogging, the crucifixion, and similar properties to fit with the person according to both natures, with the result being that the one nature, which existed prior to the incarnation, was not divine.

The Manichaeans also contended that the passage from 1 Cor. 15, "The second man from heaven," fits with the person according to both natures, so that they removed from Christ the truth of His humanity. The Church, therefore, necessarily defends and retains the synecdoche of the common participation of properties.

In this kind of proposition, the distinction is added, "according to which nature." For example, the same One is both the Son of God and the Son of Man. But "He is the Son of God according to the divinity," says Augustine, "and the Son of Man according to the humanity." This is done by the example and authority of Scripture. For example, the Son of God was born of David's seed (Rom. 1 & 9), but the phrase "according to the flesh" is added. "Christ suffered" (1 Pet. 4), but "in the flesh" is added. So in John 8, "Before Abraham was born, I am," the actual proposition is about the person. But if one asks according to which nature, one must necessarily respond, according to the divine nature.

The Manichaeans contended that Christ brought His flesh with Him from heaven, that He did not assume it from the Virgin Mary, since it is written, "The second man from heaven." But the simple and genuine response draws from this doctrine, namely, that the concrete names signify the person, not the nature; and secondly, that the actual proposition is about the person, through the common participation of properties, and the distinction is added: according to which nature.

But we must carefully observe what Cyril noted in Bk. 5 of his dialogue on this first class. The properties of the natures are not confused when they are said to be shared in common. For then would follow a confusion of the natures, which are distinguished by their properties. But just as, on account of the unity of the person, He shared in flesh and blood without conversion or confusion of the natures, so the properties of the flesh are attributed to the Word as a person. The customary rule is stated thus: The properties of one nature are not attributed to the other when considered abstractly; rather, they are shared in common with the person. Therefore, it is not said that the humanity is the divinity, for this would confuse the natures. Rather, it is said that God is Man on account of the unity of the person. In the same way, it is not said that the humanity is eternal, begotten of the Father's essence; or that the divinity was pierced with a spear or with nails. Rather, it is said that the Lord of glory was crucified, the Branch of David is Jehovah. "Nor is it right to say," says Damascenus, "that the divinity is in the flesh or that it suffered according to the flesh, but God suffered in the flesh or according to the flesh." Cyril says this: "Thus we say that God suffered, not that the Word suffered or received the holes from the nails and the other wounds by His own nature, for the divine nature cannot suffer, since it has no body."

At the Council of Chalcedon, these words were read in the epistle of Leo: "The divine nature was united to that nature which is susceptible to suffering, so that one and the same Mediator between God and men was able to die from the one, unable to die from the other." The Illyricans and Palestinians began to dispute that sentence, but the sentence of Cyril was read, plainly affirming the same thing. "The Word suffered death for us—not that the peril of death was present insofar as it pertains to His nature, for to say or to think this is astonishingly absurd—but that His flesh tasted death." The words of Cyril. Evagrius writes this, among other things, in his church history, Bk. 2, ch. 4: "The Council of Chalcedon condemns those who say that the divinity of the Only-begotten suffered." And before the fifth general council, the Church was not trivially shaken by the disputes of the Theopaschites, who contended that the divine nature itself was wounded and died, as the histories of those times reveal.

That rule of Damascenus must also be maintained: "The deeds and the sufferings are not of the natures, but of the person." That is, they are not to be attributed to only the one nature, whether divine or human, but to the person. Therefore, "it is not right to say," says Damascenus, "that the flesh of God suffered, or that the human nature in Christ died for us. But as the Nicene Creed says, the One who is of one substance with the Father came down from heaven, was crucified also for us. For although the divinity was not wounded, etc." Nevertheless, the suffering should not be relegated to the humanity alone in such a way that it is entirely removed from the divine person. For "we were not redeemed with corruptible things," says Peter (1 Pet. 1). Nor does it only pertain to God by relationship, such as, "He who touches you touches the apple of My eye." But the wounding takes place in that flesh with which the divinity is joined by the personal union, that is, the person suffers and dies.

This is what Cyril says: "To the divine nature in Christ, even now after the incarnation, is attributed the work of creation, yet not without the flesh. That is, it is attributed to that divinity which is now one person with the assumed flesh, and in this way it is attributed to the person."

There is a beautiful statement by Irenaeus which is often cited from Bk. 3, ch. 21, but it has been poorly translated, as all the writings of Irenaeus have been. For thus we read in translation: "He was Man that He might be tempted, the Word that He might be glorified, with the Word resting, that He might be tempted and dishonored and crucified and die, but with the Man being absorbed in that, that He conquers and withstands and rises again and is assumed." But Theodoret, in his third dialogue, recites that sentence of Irenaeus in Greek, as it was written by the author himself, and it is worthwhile to retain the very words of Irenaeus in the Church. His words are these: "Ὥσπερ ἦν ἄνθρωπος ἵνα πειρασθῇ, οὕτω καὶ λόγος ἵνα δοξασθῇ ἡσυχάζοντος μὲν τοῦ λόγου ἐν τῷ πειράζεσθαι καὶ σταυροῦσθαι καὶ ἀποθνήσκειν συγγινομένου δὲ τῷ ἀνθρώπῳ εν τῷ νικᾷν καὶ ὑπομένειν καὶ χρηστεύεσθαι καὶ ἀνιστάσθαι καὶ ἀναλαμβάνεσθαι. Just as He was Man that He might be tempted, so also He was the Word that He might be glorified. The Word, on the one hand, was quiet in the midst of being tempted and crucified and dying; the Word, on the other hand, was present with the Man in the midst of conquering and enduring and showing kindness and rising again and being taken up." He distinctly affirms both things: That the Word was quiet while Christ was being tempted, crucified, and dying (he uses the significant word ἡσυχάζοντος – the Word was quiet); and, at the same time, that the Word was present (namely, because of the personal union) for the nature that was suffering. The Word was not idle, but was helping that nature to be able to endure those sufferings which transcend all understanding, and to be able to conquer, rise again, ascend into heaven, and fulfill the office of the Messiah. After the conflict with the Nestorians, such forms of speaking were judged to be unhelpful—"The divine nature in Christ says or does this; the human nature in Christ says, does, suffers this." (For, as Luther says, "the division of the person necessarily follows the division of the works.") But one and the same Christ, who is here called God, there called Man, says, does, and suffers all those things, now according to the divine nature, now according to the human, now according to both natures, as will be clarified below. Nestorius did not understand this, which is why he kept saying that the Man in Christ was born, not the God who is from eternity; the Man was crucified, not the God who is impassible; similarly, that the God in Christ ruled over the winds and the sea, while the Man slept on a cushion. He says, "I admit that Christ the Man was eight days old when He was circumcised, thirty years old when He was baptized. But I will not say that the Son of God is two or three months old forever." But, in this way, he was dividing the one Christ into two persons.

This is how Luther describes the conflicts with Nestorius and Eutyches: "**Nestorius** conceded that the properties of the human nature were to be attributed to the Son of Man. **Eutyches** also attributed the properties of the divine nature to the Son of God. But they denied that common participation which attributes human properties to the Son of God and divine properties to the Son of Man. The Church, however, defends the contrary position, that there is one person who, on account of unity, is at times called God, at times Man. Not only are those propositions true that the divine properties are attributed to the Son of God, such as, 'The Son of God is the Creator, etc.,' and that the human properties are attributed to the Son of Man, such as, 'The Son of Man was hungry, slept, etc.' But those propositions are also entirely true, that the properties of the human nature are attributed to the Son of God, and in turn, the properties of the divine nature are attributed to the Son of Man. For there is one Son, one person, whether He is called God or Man, such as, 'God suffered. The Branch of David is Jehovah.'"

No one should imagine that such care for accuracy in speaking is a useless subtlety; no, Scripture itself practically dictates the words to us in order to show that the divinity is present with the suffering Christ (2 Cor. 5) in a far different way than when it says in Psalm 91, "I am with him in trouble," or as Paul says in 2 Tim. 4 that the Lord was present with him with His help. By the same token, the divinity operates in Christ differently in John 5 & 14 than it does in Romans 15. Paul says, "Which Christ has worked through me." For Peter speaks of the former works in Acts 3, "We do not do these things by our own power." Nazianzus explains these things more broadly in his epistle *Ad Clidonium*. This doctrine also shows that the suffering of Christ does not only belong to God by relationship, (Nestorius wanted to understand it this way, as Cyril reports in ch. 28, *De incarnatione unigeniti*), as Paul says that his sufferings are the sufferings of Christ (Col. 1). Otherwise, the sufferings of Christ would not surpass the sufferings of Paul, although Paul himself says (1 Cor. 1), "Was Paul crucified for you?" But it is therefore only the merit and efficacy of the death and suffering of Christ because the person of the Son of God endured it in that flesh which He made His own by the personal union, and therefore also before the incarnation. In Isaiah 50, He says, "I gave My body to those who pierce, and My cheeks to those who pull out the hair. My face I did not turn away from those who spit on Me," in order to show significantly that His suffering should be attributed to the person.

Thus it is also rightly said: "The Son of Man created heaven and earth," in order to show that the human nature has been assumed—not as Ezekiel 3 says, "The Spirit of the Lord has taken me up, etc.," but as united by a tight bond, so that there is one person. For Ezekiel is not said to be the Creator of heaven and earth, although He was taken up by the Spirit of God. But the Son of Man is called the Son of the living God, because a personal union has been made.

These things have been said about the common participation of those properties which Cyril calls "appropriated," because they are rightly attributed to the person. But they are suited to the person according to that nature of which they are proper. But one must always go on to consider what the use is of this doctrine, as we have shown very briefly.

THE SECOND CLASS

The names of the offices which are attributed to the person according to both natures.

Now, there are other properties of the offices which Cyril calls "shared in common (*communicativa*)" because, as Nazianzus says in 4. *De Theologia,* they do not belong to only one nature, as they do in the first class, but they are common to both, and for that reason also they are attributed to the person, not according to the one nature only, but according to both. To this pertains the entire mystery of redemption and the offices of the Messiah: as Mediator, Redeemer, Justifier, Life-giver, Savior, Propitiator, King, Shepherd, Priest, High Priest, etc. For if the propitiation for our sins could have been either the humanity or the divinity alone, then the Word came down from heaven "for us and for our salvation" in vain. But since the things which belong to the office of the Messiah could not be accomplished in one nature alone, either divine or human, therefore that ineffable union of the two natures was made, so that the person, in both natures and according to both natures, might work those things which pertain to our redemption.

We are not concocting this according to some dialectical division. There are clear testimonies of Scripture concerning each individual office, such as Galatians 4: "God sent His Son, made of a woman, made under law, to redeem, etc."

John 3: "He sent His only-begotten Son into the world that the world through Him might be saved."

Romans 7: "He sent His Son into the likeness of sinful flesh, that the justification of the Law might be fulfilled in us." Jeremiah 23: "I will raise up to David a righteous Branch, and this is the name which they will call Him: Jehovah our righteousness."

In these testimonies, it is expressly affirmed that the Son of God was born of a woman on account of the office of redemption; likewise, that the only-begotten Son of God was sent into the likeness of sinful flesh—that is, that the union of the two natures was made in the person of Christ—in order that the Messiah might be our righteousness and salvation.

Thus neither the divinity alone nor the humanity alone could be the Mediator between the divinity as the offended party and the human nature as the offending party, since the Mediator must be connected to both parties. Galatians 3: "A mediator is not of one." Therefore, by a wondrous combination (*temperamento*), a Mediator was made, "human divinity and divine humanity," as Augustine beautifully puts it in his homily *De ovibus*. In the same way, the testimonies should be gathered concerning the remaining offices.

From this, one can easily see how these propositions are different: Christ is the Creator, He was pierced with a spear, etc.; and Christ is the Redeemer, Justifier, etc. For the union was not made so that it could be predicated of the divine nature, that it is the Creator, and of the flesh, that it could be pierced. For those are properties of the natures, even when they are considered apart from the union. And since the natures are not confused with their own properties, these things are attributed to the person, not according to both natures, but according to that nature to which they belong. But to be the Redeemer is not a property of either nature individually, but of the office. And since the union of the two natures was made on account of that office, as we have already shown, therefore it also applies to the person, not according to one nature alone, but according to both.

But let us learn to understand rightly that mode of speaking, namely, "according to both natures," that the person acts in these offices, not in one nature only, but that the person performs actions in both natures at the same time.

For example, to the office of redemption pertain two things: **first**, to suffer, to die, etc. (Luke 24). These actions are properly done in the human nature.

Second, to conquer death through suffering (Heb. 2), to restore eternal life (John 10). These actions are proper to the divine nature, but they are not done separately, so that the humanity acts separately in suffering and the divinity acts separately in the destruction of death. No, they are united, just as to the nature itself, in one person, and thus together they accomplish the work of redemption.

From this, it can be understood how necessary it is that the proposition be retained in the Church: "Christ is the Redeemer according to both natures." For we believe that the divine nature in Christ was not idle in the work of redemption while the person was working only in the human nature. But (as Damascenus says, and his saying was most agreeable to those who came after him) that "one nature acts with the common participation of the other." For the synonyms are used by the Fathers, of which the one is clarified by the other. The person acts according to both natures. The person performs actions in both natures at once. And one nature acts with the common participation of the other. This mode of speaking was accepted and approved at the Council of Chalcedon.

To this pertains the sentence of Irenaeus which we cited above in which it is clear how carefully antiquity spoke about these great mysteries. He says, "He was Man that He might be tempted, and the Word that He might be glorified." You will observe how elegantly Irenaeus explains what we customarily say: "According to both natures." For, he says, "συγγινομένου δὲ τῷ ἀνθρώπῳ εν τῷ νικᾶν - the Word, on the other hand, was present with the Man in the midst of the conquering, etc."

In the sixth council, the saying of Gregory of Nyssa is cited: "The suffering indeed belongs to the body of Christ, but the fact that we are saved by it is the working of God." That is, as we ourselves speak, one nature acts with the common participation of the other. And since, in the weighty exercises of repentance and faith, one must ponder the offices of Christ, therefore antiquity splendidly observed about the miracles how one nature acts with the common participation of the other. In Matthew 8, the Savior heals a leper by touch. In Luke 7, He touches the coffin and the dead man arises. In Mark 6, He takes the girl by the hand and raises her. In Mark 7, He puts His finger into the ears, touches the tongue, and heals, etc.

Naturally, He could have performed all these things with a word alone, but He wanted to employ His flesh, that He might reveal its dignity, lest anyone should contend that there was no use for Christ's flesh as a created thing in divine blessings as immense as redemption, justification, etc. For the divinity does not have in its nature a finger to put into the ears, nor a hand with which to raise the girl, but it uses the assumed flesh for this purpose, and that contact, in turn, shares (*participat,* as the Scholastics speak) the power of the divinity, so that it can heal the deaf, give life to the girl. Thus since the death of the Mediator was needed to intercede (Heb. 9), and since the divinity in its own nature could not die, it assumed the humanity for this purpose. And that suffering, in turn, shares the power of the divinity. This is why He is able to conquer death and restore eternal life, for otherwise the suffering of the whole world are not worthy of the future glory (Rom. 8).

One should also remember the comparison of red-hot iron, which the Church at all times has used on many occasions to clarify this class of properties. The wood is branded with the red-hot iron, and since there are two substances there, one asks, is that branding done by the iron or by the fire? But clearly this cannot be done either by the fire on its own or by the iron on its own. The iron is heated with fire so that the branding may be done, in which the iron does not act separately in penetrating, nor does the fire act separately in burning, but it burns as it penetrates and it penetrates as it burns. And so in the red-hot iron one substance acts with the common participation of the other. The iron, in its nature, has the power to press, but the fire shares with it its ability to burn as it presses. The fire, for its part, has power to burn, but that it makes an impression as it burns is due to the iron that shares its property with it. The application of this comparison is easy and clear and beautifully illustrates this whole teaching. There is good reason why it was so popular in the whole of antiquity.

Two things, then, must be noted in this class when we say,

"according to both natures." **First**, that the union of the two natures into one person of Christ was made for the sake of accomplishing those offices. **Second**, that the person performs actions in these offices in both natures at once, and yet neither of them acts separately, but the one with the common participation of the other, as has already been clarified.

This consideration will become more delightful when we not only learn from the rules, but when we carefully observe those things in the very words of Scripture and put them to serious use in consolation. Hebrews 2 is a beautiful passage. In order to destroy that strong man who held the power over death, it was necessary for a stronger man to come along, namely, God Himself. But since that had to happen through death, and since God in His own nature cannot suffer, therefore the text says, "He was made a partaker of flesh and blood, that He might destroy death and deliver, etc." John 10: "The good Shepherd lays down His life for the sheep and gives them eternal life." Those two things are not befitting to a single nature, either the divine or the human. Therefore, the union of both natures into one person was made. Hebrews 9: "The blood of Christ, who through the eternal Spirit offered Himself unblemished to God, cleanses the conscience from dead works." This passage beautifully demonstrates how one nature acts with the common participation of the other.

But it is manifestly false when some cry out that antiquity always attributes all the predicated things to Christ, either according to the divine nature alone, or to the human nature alone. For Cyril expressly repeats in many places that certain sayings of the Gospel apply to the divinity, certain things to the humanity; that certain things are in the middle, with a view toward both the divinity and the humanity at the same time, etc.

There is a beautiful statement of Epiphanius in Vol. 2, Bk. 23. "We do not place our hope or trust in man, since 'cursed is he who confides in man.' Therefore, the divinity and the humanity were one when Christ suffered in the flesh, so that we have justification not only in the flesh, but also in the divinity, so that salvation might result for us both in the divinity and in the flesh.

Damascenus, Bk. 3, ch. 19:"It is the same to say that Christ acts according to both natures, and that each nature acts in Christ with the common participation of the other."

But a certain consideration of the important matters is altogether necessary, for in this way the doctrine is elucidated concerning the benefits of the Son of God, and, in a certain way, we can understand from this the magnitude of sin, that the human race could be delivered from the slavery of sin and death in no other way except that the Son of God should, through death, destroy the power of death (Heb. 2). And 1 Pet. 1,"You were not redeemed with perishable things."

Rom. 5: Our Mediator not only died for us, but we are also saved from wrath through His life.

Rom. 8: We conquer not only because of Him, but also through Him who loved us.

I am intentionally passing by many disputes from the fifth and sixth councils on the two wills and the two actions in Christ, although they can easily be evaluated from these foundations, with just a little effort.

Schwenckfeldt prattles that extraordinary idolatry is committed if the humanity of Christ is worshiped together with the divinity with equal adoration, since it is a created thing. But from these foundations, the true and firm response is drawn. We call upon Christ as Mediator, Redeemer, Savior, etc. But we have shown that these offices apply to the person according to both natures. Therefore, when a person calls upon Him, the mind should not separate the human nature from that person who is invoked, since invocation should expressly keep the benefits of Christ in view, which He furnished for us in both natures.

Cyril elegantly says, "We were baptized into the Father, the Son, and the Holy Spirit, ὁμοουσίους—of the same substance, and yet we were not baptized only into the divine nature of the Son, since we were baptized into His death" (Rom. 6).

Basil says, "We must believe, glorify, and invoke, in the same way as we were baptized."

THE THIRD CLASS

On account of the personal union with the divinity, Scripture predicates many things of the human nature in Christ which in no way fit with the properties of our bodies.

The human nature does not dwell in Christ as it does in one of the saints. Rather, He has joined to Himself that mass of the human nature with a very tight bond, which we signify in some way when we refer to it as the "personal union." Moreover, the manner of this union is clarified in some way with the customary comparison: As fire penetrates iron and is mixed with it on all sides, so the Word, in assuming the human nature, glows in all of it, and the human nature, like a lamp that has been lit, is united to the Word. This is what Paul meant to convey when he said that "in Christ dwells the fullness of the divinity σωματικῶς – bodily." For he intended to demonstrate without any doubt this difference: that the bodies of believers are indeed temples of the indwelling Holy Spirit. And yet Paul rightly says, "I know that in my flesh nothing good dwells, I feel another law in my members, etc." But in Christ, the divinity dwells bodily in such a way that the very body of Christ is full of the divinity, just as in red-hot iron no part of the iron is without the fire.

Therefore, since Scripture affirms both things, our faith believes them: **First**, that Christ was made like His brothers in all things except for sin. For He assumed a human body with those properties which pertain to the condition and genuineness of the human nature.

Second, our faith also learns this from Scripture, that, on account of the personal union with the divinity, the human nature in Christ has many peculiar prerogatives and conditions (or if someone prefers to use another word, I will not contend over terms) in that person which it does not have apart from that union, when it is considered in our bodies. For only that mass has been joined by personal union to the divinity, so that the Word glows in the whole mass. Only that mass has been exalted to the right hand of the power and majesty of God. Scripture expressly explains what that exaltation is in 1 Peter 3: "Who has gone to the right hand of God in heaven, with angels and authorities and powers having been placed under Him." Eph. 1: "Seating Him at His right hand in the heavens, above all principality, authority, dominion, and every name which is named, not only in this age, but also in the one to come, and has placed all things under His feet, etc." And in 1 Cor. 11, Paul certainly does not make Christ equal to God according to the human nature, for he says, "The Head of Christ is God" (for the humanity is not converted into divinity). But since a personal union was made, he places the human nature in Christ far above and beyond the rank of all other creatures. For He is the Head, not only of woman and man (1 Cor. 11), but also of powers, dominions, etc. (1 Pet. 3), and above every name also in the age to come (Eph. 1). Luke 10: "All things have been delivered to Me by My Father." Mat. 28: "All authority in heaven and on earth has been given to Me." In that statement from John 5, "The Father has given the Son to have life in Himself," Cyril skillfully weighs what follows, "because He is the Son of Man," and affirms that the human nature, on its own, apart from that union, does not have life in itself, but from that personal union with the divinity, it has been made a Life-giver.

Therefore, it is certain and clear that in the human nature of Christ, there is not only the first class of properties, in which He is like His brothers, but on account of the union with the divinity, the flesh of Christ has many prerogatives in addition to and beyond the condition and properties of our bodies.

Moreover, this reminder must always be added and diligently inculcated when discussing this doctrine: That one must not, by private judgment, weave together all kinds of consequences from that prerogative of the personal union, as some contended in former times that the body of Christ, on account of the union with the Word, was immune from pain while He suffered, even as rust cannot eat into red-hot iron.

The Manichaeans also imagined that Christ did not truly die, since death cannot cause that body to decay which is full of life-giving life. But this is the status of this doctrine: When Scripture predicates something of Christ's body which is not found among the properties of our bodies, we should neither deny nor elude it with the pretext that He is like His brothers in all things. Rather, our faith should simply believe when Scripture attributes something to Christ's body, even if it goes beyond the condition and properties of our bodies. For only this mass was personally united to the divinity. It alone has been placed at the right hand of the power and majesty of God.

That first class of properties in which He is similar to His brothers is more notable and can be more easily understood, because, from a consideration of our own nature, we can judge in a certain way what the properties of the body of Christ are in which He is similar to His brothers. But this third class is not so easily recognized, because in the whole nature of things, there is no similar example. Therefore, testimonies of Scripture must be gathered that demonstrate which things are rightly attributed to the human nature in Christ in this third class.

We will note some things. Eph. 1: "We have redemption in His blood." Rom. 5: "In His blood we have been justified." 1 John 3: "His blood cleanses us from all our sins." Isa. 53: "By His bruise we are healed." John 6: "My flesh it is which I will give for the life of the world." Surely we cannot attribute these things to the nature of any man, even the holiest of men, without extraordinary idolatry! How, then, do we believe such things about the body and blood of Christ when Scripture affirms them? How is it that we are obligated to believe such things under peril of our salvation, if, according to His human nature, He is merely like His brothers in all things?

Nestorius also held this error, among others, that he denied that the flesh of Christ is life-giving, because that is not a property of the human nature in our bodies, and Christ is supposed to be like His brothers in all things according to His humanity. But the Council of Ephesus rightly says that the flesh by itself and by its own nature, apart from that union, cannot give life; but that Christ's flesh, to which the divine nature is united in such a way that the divinity of the Word glows personally in His entire flesh, as by a lamp that has been lit, has actually become life-giving by that union. In a similar way, iron, by its nature, does not glow, does not burn. But when it is heated by fire, then it obtains those properties, both of glowing and of burning. Thus all human bodies, when the soul departs, according to the laws of physics, necessarily see corruption. But after Christ's spirit was expelled from His body, His body not only did not see corruption, but as Peter says in Acts 2, "It was impossible, etc.," because (as Athanasius says about the incarnation of the Word) "the divinity dwells in that body personally." Therefore, the body of Christ is like His brothers in all things in this way, that at the same time, because of the union, it obtains an immense difference. For the corruption which necessarily happens in our bodies is impossible in the body of Christ on account of the union with the divinity.

Jerome says that in Luke 24, when the body of Christ disappeared, it is not the body of a shadow or a ghost, but it is the power of God.

In disputing the walking of Christ's body upon the waters, Jerome says that it does not detract from the truth of the human nature. "Not the loss of the nature, but the power of God is displayed."

Augustine, Tractate 121 on John: "The closed doors did not hinder the mass of the body where divinity was." The author of the questions which are reported in the name of Justin also raises this question: How did the Lord go in to His disciples with the doors closed? Was the stone rolled away by the ministry of the angel so that He could go out of the tomb with His body? He responds: "Just as He walked on water by divine power, without emptying His body, so also by His own divine power He went out of the tomb before the stone was rolled away. For the stone was not rolled away by the angel so that Christ could rise, but so that those who came to the tomb could see the linen cloths and the face cloth, the most obvious signs of the resurrection. In the same way," he says, "He went in to the disciples with the doors closed, for He presented His body to be touched in order to show that He had not gone in to them with the doors closed as a spirit, but in the body, by His divine power, that is, that He can do and furnish those things which are beyond nature." And he signifies with prerogatives of this kind that nothing was detracted from the truth of the human nature in Christ, for he says, "The things which are beyond nature are done in nature according to divine power, etc."

Nazianzus says, "Just as the sun is touched by a cloud, and is and remains a shining body, even though it does not cast its rays abroad, so at the time of the exinanition the divinity was quiet in the human nature of Christ in such a way that no prerogative appeared ahead of our bodies." But in the transfiguration, as Augustine elegantly puts it, it was as if rays of divinity suddenly appeared in that body when His face shone like the sun.

Here we can also bring in that saying which John, with great solemnity, remembers as something extraordinary: that blood and water flowed from the side of the already dead body of Christ. "He who saw it has testified, and his testimony is true. And he knows that the things he says are true, that you also may believe." [John 19]

This, too, is clear, that this third class was not unknown to the ancients. For Cyril says, *De vera fide ad Reginas,* "The Word is accustomed to making common the benefits of His nature with His own body." Cyril, *De incarnatione*: "Since it is the only-begotten God's own body, it transcends all things human." The same, in *Joannem,* Bk. 4, ch. 12: "The life-giving nature of the Word, by that ineffable manner of union, joined to the flesh, made the flesh life-giving." In the same place: "The flesh, understood according to itself, cannot give life. But if you consider the mystery of the incarnation, forasmuch as the flesh can do nothing on its own, nevertheless you will not doubt that it has become life-giving, for it is not the flesh of just anyone, but of the Life itself, our Savior Jesus Christ, in whom the fullness of the Deity dwells bodily." Therefore, this is the understanding of the Fathers: That Christ, according to His humanity, is like His brothers in all things in such a way that His body, nevertheless, also transcends all things human at the same time.

Augustine, *De incarnatione,* cites Psalm 45 in favor of this understanding: "Your God has anointed You ahead of Your companions, etc."

Damascenus, Bk. 3, ch. 7: "We say that the natures of the Lord pass into themselves, and yet the passing originates in the divine nature, for it passes through all things, while nothing passes through it. Indeed, the divine nature itself passes on its own glorifications to the flesh, and yet it remains immune to the sufferings of the flesh." And in ch. 17: "The flesh of the Lord, enriched with divine actions on account of the union, does not endure the disappearance of the natural properties, but it works divine things because the Word has been united to it, as red-hot iron burns, not because of its nature, etc." Likewise: "It was mortal on account of itself, life-giving on account of the personal union." But as for human reason, it often clashes with this and is offended with thoughts about the likeness to our bodies; this is not new. For there are several examples of this kind noted in the Scriptures, so that by them minds are fortified ahead of time and instructed.

In the story in Matthew 14, Mark 6, and John 6, the body of Christ walks upon the waves of the roaring sea and does not sink. Now, the disciples knew that the body of the Savior was like His brothers in all things except for sin, and for this reason, although they recognized Him, they thought He was a ghost, because it is not a property of the human body to be able to walk on water and not sink. But Christ refutes those thoughts, saying, "It is I!" And in order to show that this did not detract from the genuineness of His body, He commands Peter to come to Him upon the water. For if the word of Christ can cause this in Peter's body, so that, contrary to the properties of the human body, he walks on water, why, then, would we reduce to a lesser condition the human nature in Christ, which is personally united to the divinity? So also, when Scripture affirms something about the body of Christ, we do not want to believe, because it does not agree with the condition of our bodies. But we must carefully note what Matthew adds: "Those who were in the boat came and worshiped Him, saying, 'Truly You are the Son of God!'" For earlier they only considered that class of properties in which He is like His brothers, and from that they concluded that it could not be the body of Christ which they saw walking upon the waves. But afterwards they say, "Truly You are the Son of God"; that is, they learn to see the body of Christ insofar as it is united to the divinity, and on account of that union, they acknowledge that other more excellent properties are befit Him.

In the same way, the property of human bodies does not admit the penetration of dimensions, so much so that it is one of the impossibilities, as all physical scientists agree and as universal experience testifies. And yet, when the doors were closed for fear of the Jews, Jesus stood with His body in the midst of the disciples. And lest they should doubt, He said, "It is I!" But since they were troubled and terrified, the text says that they thought they were seeing a ghost, because it is not a property of the human body to enter through closed doors; the genuineness of the body, by reason of physics, cannot stand alongside the penetration of dimensions. It is no wonder, therefore, that argumentations about the genuineness of the human body, even now, incite such great tumults in the Sacramentarian affair, for they had so seized the minds of the disciples that, contrary to the manifest word of Christ, who said, "It is I!", which could not be eluded by any figure of speech—indeed, contrary to their very sense of sight—although they saw His body standing in the midst, they thought that it could not be the true body of the Savior. For it is not a property of a true body suddenly to stand in the midst with the doors closed; this is a property of ghosts. But Christ affirms with a long speech that this does not detract from the genuineness of His body. For this reason, He presents His flesh and bones to be touched and seen, and He eats in their presence, etc.

These things must be observed on account of the Zwinglians. For although Christ affirms with express words that His body and blood are present in the Supper, they deny this, because it is a property of our bodies not to be able to be in more than one place at a time. And "Christ is like His brothers in all things." Likewise, according to the manner of a true body, the body of Christ cannot be present in heaven and in the Supper at the same time, although the Word of God clearly affirms, "This is My body." But those examples which we have demonstrated from clear foundations of Scripture show that it does not detract from the genuineness of the human nature in Christ when the Word of God predicates something of the body of Christ which does not fit with the properties of our bodies. This can be correctly understood from the comparison of red-hot iron. For red-hot iron, on account of the union with the fire, has two sets of properties. **First**, those things which iron tends to have by its own nature. **Second**, in addition to those things, it obtains certain peculiarities from the fire which iron does not otherwise have by its own nature, such as to glow, to burn. And yet the red-hot iron both is and remains genuine iron, even after the fire is added. No sane person argues as follows: "It is not the property of iron to glow or to burn. Therefore, the red-hot iron does not glow, does not burn, for iron has some properties of its own, whereas red-hot iron has other properties." Indeed, even in our body this can be considered, for insofar as it is animated, it has far different properties than if it were considered by itself, apart from the union with the soul. For in a body from which the soul is separated, the villi neither attract nor retain nor expel, and yet these are properties of an animated body.

Moreover, I now repeat at the end what I said before. We do not seek with this doctrine to confuse the natures. It was clearly demonstrated in the first class why the natures are distinguished by properties. Nor do we teach that, on account of the personal union with the divinity, anyone can arbitrarily imagine whatever he wants about the body of Christ. But this is the understanding: We should believe the Scripture when it speaks about the body of Christ, not only when it affirms that Christ, according to the human nature, is like His brothers in all things except for sin, but when the Word of God predicates something of Christ's humanity which does not harmonize with our bodies, but is foreign to their condition and far exceeds and surpasses their properties, lest we either deny or elude what Scripture says. But let us ponder the words of Cyril: "Since it is the only-begotten God's own body, it transcends all things human."

Leipzig
in the workshop of M. Ernesti Voegelini Constantiensis
in the year 1561

Scripture References

Old Testament

Daniel

Jonah

Zechariah

New Testament

Matthew

Mark

Luke

John

Acts

Hebrews

1 Peter

2 Peter

1 John

Jude

References to the Church Fathers and Theologians through Bernard of Clairvaux

Made in the USA
Las Vegas, NV
26 February 2022

44615344R00125